ELEMENTS
OF MODERN PHILOSOPHY

ELEMENTS OF MODERN PHILOSOPHY: DESCARTES THROUGH KANT

WILLIAM H. BRENNER

Old Dominion University

Prentice Hall
Englewood Cliffs, New Jersey 07632

Library of Congress Cataloging-in-Publication Data

BRENNER, WILLIAM H. (Date)
  The elements of modern philosophy.

  Includes bibliographies and index.
  1. Philosophy, Modern. 2. Philosophy, European—
History. I. Title.
B791.B74 1988   190   88-2485
ISBN 0-13-268137-4

Editorial/production supervision and
  interior design: Mary Araneo
Cover art: William Blake, *Europe, A Prophecy* frontispiece. Fitzwilliam Museum, University of
Cambridge, England.
Cover design: Wanda Lubelska Design
Manufacturing buyer: Peter Havens
Photo credits: p. 1, *Galileo;* p. 9, *Descartes* (New York Public Library
Picture Collection); p. 25, *Spinoza;* p. 40, *Leibniz* (New York Public
Library Picture Collection); p. 54, *Locke;* p. 75, *Berkeley* (New York Public
Library Picture Collection); p. 90, *Hume* (New York Public Library Picture Collection);
p. 119. *Kant* (New York Public Library Picture Collection).

Printed in the United States of America

10 9 8 7 6 5 4 3 2 1

ISBN 0-13-268137-4

Prentice-Hall International (UK) Limited, *London*
Prentice-Hall of Australia Pty. Limited, *Sydney*
Prentice-Hall Canada Inc., *Toronto*
Prentice-Hall Hispanoamericana, S.A., *Mexico*
Prentice-Hall of India Private Limited, *New Delhi*
Prentice-Hall of Japan, Inc., *Tokyo*
Simon & Schuster Asia Pte. Ltd., *Singapore*
Editora Prentice-Hall do Brasil, Ltda., *Rio de Janeiro*

For Emily and William

CONTENTS

PREFACE

The history of Western philosophy is generally divided into three major periods: *ancient* (sixth century B.C. through fifth century A.D.), *medieval* (sixth century through fifteenth century), and *modern* (seventeenth century through the present).[1] This book deals with the seminal thinkers of the modern epoch, namely the great scientist-philosophers of seventeenth- and eighteenth-century Europe.

Though influenced in many ways by their medieval predecessors, these thinkers of the early modern period were true revolutionaries, who successfully challenged the dominance of medieval ways of thought and who initiated a new tradition of philosophical investigation. In initiating this new tradition, they formulated a set of problems which remains to this day the focus of philosophical education and research.

This book is an introduction to those problems as they are expressed and answered and debated in the works of Descartes, Spinoza, Leibniz, Locke, Berkeley, Hume, and Kant. Somewhat special emphasis is placed on Descartes, Hume, and Kant—arguably the most important figures of the classical period of modern philosophy.

[1]The sixteenth century, the time of the High Renaissance and the Reformation, is considered a transitional period.

Readers are asked to study the present book in conjunction with some complete classic texts. Especially recommended are Descartes' *Meditations,* Hume's *Enquiry Concerning Human Understanding,* and Hume's *Dialogues Concerning Natural Religion.* Their importance is matched by their readability, and each is available in inexpensive paperback editions.

Except for the chapters on Descartes and Hume, each chapter contains an excerpt from a classic text along with my own expository and interpretive introduction. Each chapter concludes with a set of questions designed to promote review, discussion, and criticism of the preceding text and to suggest paper topics.

My aim has been to write a sound and accessible introduction to the metaphysics and epistemology of early modern philosophy, an introduction that is concise and perspicuous as well as substantive and challenging. For the most part, I have refrained from critiquing the theses and arguments of the philosophers, believing that this important and interesting task is best left to the reader. May this book prepare the way for relevant critical discussion of the classic texts.

My interpretive remarks are indebted to works by many scholars, especially those mentioned in the bibliography at the end of each chapter. I want to acknowledge a special debt to individuals who commented on parts of my manuscript, including Jonathan Bennett, D.C. Yalden-Thomson, George Thomas, M.J. Ferreira, Harry Jones, Lewis Ford, Leemon McHenry, Lee C. Rice, Warren Funk, David Loomis, David James, Vincent Vaccaro, William G. Dyer, and Fred Westphal. These readers helped me to weed out many errors and infelicities. (Similar help from you, the present reader, would be welcome.) Finally, I want to thank Old Dominion University's College of Arts and Letters for a generous grant in support of my research in modern philosophy.

William H. Brenner

ELEMENTS
OF MODERN PHILOSOPHY

introduction

DEMOCRITUS TO GALILEO

MODERN PHILOSOPHY

Philosophy is the inquiry into fundamental principles. At its center are *metaphysics* and *epistemology*. Metaphysics seeks the fundamental principles of *reality;* epistemology, the fundamental principles of our *knowledge* of reality.

    Modern philosophy can be usefully characterized as the investigation of the metaphysical and epistemological problems generated by reflection on modern science. It can be seen as the still-continuing effort to understand the foundations, implications, and limitations of the revolutionary conception developed in seventeenth-century European science—the conception of the natural world as a system of matter governed by mechanical laws and knowable only through mathematical analysis.

ATOMISM

This modern conception of nature had been anticipated, in part, by the Greek atomist Democritus (born around 460 B.C.):

> By convention there is sweet, by convention there is bitter, by convention hot
> and cold, by convention color; but in reality there are only atoms and the
> void.[1]

But it was only in the seventeenth century, through the work of the Italian
mathematician Galileo Galilei (1564–1642), that atomism came alive and
began to exert widespread influence. Using mathematical methods of analysis, Galileo was able to apply it fruitfully to concrete physical problems.
Through this work he was to earn the title Father of Modern Physics.

Following Democritus, Galileo maintained that natural objects are to
be understood in terms of their directly measurable properties, namely
their shape, quantity, and motion. He contrasted these properties—the so-
called *primary qualities*—with odor, taste, sound, color, warmth, or coldness—
the so-called *secondary qualities*. These secondary qualities are not really qualities *of objects* at all, according to Galileo:

> I think that tastes, odours, colours, and so on are no more than mere names
> so far as the objects in which we locate them are concerned, and that they
> reside only in consciousness. If living creatures were removed, all these quali-
> ties would be wiped out and annihilated.[2]

The secondary qualities are ascribed to physical objects *by convention*
(as Democritus had put it), while the primary qualities belong to them *by
nature*. The primary qualities are the *real* properties of objects, belonging to
even those which are too small to be sensed; the secondary qualities are
merely *apparent* properties of objects, being in fact sensations caused in us
by the impact of atoms on our sense organs.

Suppose that one person, sticking his hand into some water, says "It's
hot!" while another, sticking her hand into the same water, says "It's cold!"
Which is right? This old riddle—a real problem for the established science
of Galileo's day—was easily resolved in Galileo's science through the use of
the distinction between "the way water feels to us" (hot or cold) and the
"objective truth about it" (its temperature).[3] The scientific concept of temperature allows us to make a (right or wrong) judgment about a quality
really residing in the water, while the common, unscientific notion (hot or
cold) does not. This is because the scientific concept, unlike the ordinary
one, is clear and distinct, being defined in terms of the directly measurable
"primary" qualities alone.

SCHOLASTICISM

The established science of Galileo's day—the official doctrine of the schools
or universities—was known as Scholasticism. Scholastic doctrine included
a science of nature, a science its professors had learned from medieval com-

mentaries on works of Aristotle and which they defended by reference to Aristotle's authority as "the master of those who know" (*il maestro di color che sanno,* in the beautiful Italian of Dante).[4]

The old riddle mentioned earlier was a real problem for the Scholastics. According to Galileo and other moderns, this was because of their uncritical reliance on the evidence of the senses and (a related point) because of their tendency to project their own sensations onto natural objects. Because of their so-called naive realism, they developed no systematic method of distinguishing real from merely apparent qualities of objects; because of their habit of reading the contents of consciousness into natural reality, they persisted in teaching a fruitless approach to nature—the so-called physics of final causes.

We need to look at both of these criticisms in turn, starting with the second.

FINAL CAUSALITY

A notorious example of how the Scholastics explained things is their account of why a stone falls to the ground when dropped: "It falls to the ground because it seeks its natural place near the center of the earth." Modern thinkers saw this as a mistake based on uncritical projection of human goal-directedness onto inanimate nature—a mistake fostered by uncritical faith in Aristotle's doctrine of the four causes. We need to understand this doctrine in order to understand modern thought.

According to Aristotle, all natural substances, as well as all products of human art, are to be explained in tems of two intrinsic factors and two extrinsic factors. The two intrinsic factors are the material cause and the formal cause.

The *material cause* of a thing is "that out of which it is made." We appeal to this sort of cause when we explain the fact that not all fabrics burn by saying that some fabrics are made of asbestos.

The *formal cause* of something is its "form," i.e., the kind of thing it is. We appeal to formal cause when we explain the fact that a certain knife cuts hardwood by saying it is a *sharp* knife; or when we explain why the square on the longest side of a given triangle is equal to the sum of the squares on the other two sides, by saying that it is a *right* triangle.

The two extrinsic factors are the efficient and the final causes.

The *efficient cause* is the agency responsible for bringing something into being, or for maintaining its being. Thus we explain the melting of a piece of wax by referring to the action of a flame, and explain its persistence in the liquid state by reference to the continuing presence of the flame.

The *final cause* of something is the purpose for which it was made or accomplished, or the *function* which it serves in relation to some end (*telos*).

We appeal to a final cause when we explain why a knife is made the way it is by referring to its intended function, or when we explain why organisms with blood have hearts by referring to the organism's need for a steady circulation of oxygenated blood, etc. These are known as *teleological explanations*.

According to Aristotle and his Scholastic followers, the final cause is "the cause of causes." For it is the final cause (the goal) which defines the efficient cause's activity and directs its choice of materials and form. Therefore (they continued), the search for final causes must be the primary activity of scientists, i.e., of those who would know the causes of things.

The assumption is that *all* things act for an end, an assumption that implies that all adequate explanations, in natural science as well as in human art, must be primarily teleological.

It was against that fundamental assumption of Aristotelian-Scholastic philosophy that the early modern thinkers[5] rebelled most passionately. For it seemed to express a totally fruitless and obscurantic conception of nature and of natural science, a conception which blocked the way of progress. What the Scholastics gave out as scientific explanation was really, according to their modern critics, either true but empty redescriptions of natural phenomena, for example,

> Stones fall to the earth because they are heavy (where "heavy" simply means "tend to fall to the earth"),

or else baseless and obscurantic attributions of "occult" psychological powers and conscious states to the natural world, for example,

> Stones fall to the earth because they are *seeking* their natural place.

According to the moderns, what we need in natural science is a precise description of *how* stones fall, rather than a vague explanation of *why* they fall. What we need is mathematical analysis, not teleological explanation. And so we must approach natural things by measuring their directly measurable features (primary qualities), rather than by projecting into them hidden (occult) teleological powers.

DIRECT REALISM

So the early moderns regarded the Scholastics' statement, "The stone falls to the earth because it seeks its natural place" as a mistake—the mistake of projecting human volition (seeking, choosing, intending) onto human nature. They likewise regarded such everyday statements as "The water is hot" and "The rose is red" as mistakes—mistakes of ascribing human sensations to insensitive objects. And these "everyday mistakes" they traced to people's innately uncritical reliance on sense experience—a reliance that can be moderated only through rigorous scientific education.

The tendency toward blind faith in the senses was actually reinforced by the theory of perception commonly taught by Scholastic philosophers, the theory known as *direct realism,* or *naive realism.* This is the theory that physical objects and their qualities are *directly* present to us in our sense experience of them. An example of a physical object and its qualities would be a particular table and its specific color, shape, etc. Direct realists say that all knowledge of the physical world must be based on *direct* perception of such *real* (i.e., physical) objects and qualities. They insist that our primary knowledge of these things comes to us directly, through seeing or otherwise sensing them, rather than indirectly, through inferring their existence from something else.

The Scholastics used Aristotle's matter/form distinction to explain how the direct perception of physical things is possible. They explained that, in seeing an object, our "sensitive faculties" (powers of sensing) are being imprinted with the actual *form* of the object (i.e., its nature and qualities). This imprinted form they called a "sensible species." The sensible species is the form of an object *as present to a perceiving mind.* It is present to a knowing mind "in abstraction from the matter" of the object. For example: The perceiving mind does not become a brown object when it perceives the brownness of the desk. Another example: The *mind,* in perceiving a table-top, doesn't receive the form *squareness* in the manner in which *lumber,* in the process of making a table, receives a square shape.

THE NEW WAY OF IDEAS

Objections to Direct Realism

Drawing on recently rediscovered texts from the ancient Greek Skeptics, early modern thinkers developed several arguments against the direct, or "naive" realist view of sense perception, one of which, known as *the argument from relativity,* went as follows:

> Physical objects and their qualities do not vary with the point of view or mental state of the perceiver.
>
> But what is directly and immediately present to the perceiver in sense experience *does* vary with the point of view and mental state of the perceiver.
>
> Therefore (*contra* naive realism), physical objects and their qualities are not directly present to the perceiver in sense experience.[6]

Accepting the conclusion of this argument, namely that the direct objects of perception are never *physical* particulars, modern philosophers drew the further conclusion that they must be *mental* particulars:

> *Something* is directly and immediately present to us in sense experience.
> This "something" is either physical or mental.
> It is not physical.
> Therefore, it is mental.

With this argument, philosophy had embarked on what John Locke was to call its "New Way of Ideas." For *ideas* was the name commonly given to the "mental somethings"—sensations and images—which were supposed to be the only direct objects of perception.

The old way of doing natural science (Scholasticism) was thought to be based on a systematic failure to distinguish *things as they really are* from *things as they appear to us*, i.e., a failure to distinguish *things* from our *ideas* of things. The New Way of Ideas was to be the basis of a new, more critical way of doing natural science. The essence of this new way would be the method by which it distinguishes the real (objective) features of things from the merely apparent (subjective) features. And this method was to be the one devised by Galileo and based on the following *criterion of measurability:* Only the measurable qualities (primary qualities) are real, exist in things; all others are merely apparent, exist only in our idea of things.

An Alternative to Direct Realism

If *ideas* are the only objects of human perception, then how do we ever come to know anything about *things?* This question, known as *the problem of perception,* was answered by most early modern thinkers as follows:

> It is true that we do not really (i.e., directly) perceive physical objects. But we really perceive *representations* (ideas) of physical objects.
> These representations are *caused* by the action of physical objects on our faculty of sensation.
> Some representations are totally "impressionistic"—they bear no resemblance to what they represent. Such are the ideas of the secondary qualities.
> Some are realistic likenesses of what they represent. Such are the ideas of the primary qualities.

This answer to the problems of perception bears the name *representational realism.* It is called *realism* because it says that we do have knowledge of real objects, existing independently of the mind; it is called *representational* because it says that our only knowledge of this reality is indirect, coming by way of inference from certain representations which are directly present to the mind in perception.

Representational realism is a theory of perception that was congenial to the mathematical physics emerging in the seventeenth century. But was it a *true* theory? In the following chapter we shall be studying the work of a philosopher who claimed to demonstrate the truth of representational realism and to thereby provide for modern physics a secure metaphysical foundation.

FOR FURTHER READING

On the Topics of This Introduction

E. A. BURTT, *The Metaphysical Foundations of Modern Physical Science.* New York: Doubleday, 1955.
STILLMAN DRAKE, *Galileo.* New York: Hill & Wang, 1980.
ROBERT G. OLSON, "The Nature and Existence of the External World," in Chapter 2 in *A Short Introduction to Philosophy,* New York: Harcourt, Brace, & World, 1967. I am particularly indebted to this work.
RICHARD H. POPKIN, *The History of Skepticism from Erasmus to Descartes.* New York: Harper & Row, 1968.

General

WALLACE I. MATSON, *A New History of Philosophy,* Vol. II. New York: Harcourt Brace Jovanovich, 1987.
ROGER SCRUTON, *From Descartes to Wittgenstein: A Short History of Modern Philosophy.* London: Rutledge & Kegan Paul, 1981.
PAUL EDWARDS, ed., *The Encyclopedia of Philosophy.* New York: Macmillan, 1967. The standard reference work in philosophy.
A. R. LACEY, *A Dictionary of Philosophy.* New York: Scribner's, 1976.
WILLIAM BARRETT, *Death of the Soul.* Garden City, N.Y.: Doubleday, 1986. An intriguing critical discussion of modern thought.

QUESTIONS

1. *Define:* philosophy, modern philosophy, primary and secondary qualities, atomism.

2. Using examples of your own, explain Aristotle's doctrine of the four causes.

3. Contrast Galileo's approach to physics with that of Aristotle and the Scholastics.

4. *Explain:* direct realism, the New Way of Ideas, the problems of perception, representational realism.

5. What led Galileo to the conclusion that "colors and so on are no more than mere names . . . "? Do you agree with his reasoning?

NOTES

[1]From Philip Wheelwright, trans., *The Presocratics* (New York: Odyssey, 1966).

[2]Quoted on p. 70 of Stillman Drake's *Galileo* (New York: Hill & Wang, 1980). The translation is by Drake himself.

[3]Here I have borrowed material from Susan Khin Zaw's *John Locke: The Foundations of Empiricism* (Milton Keynes, England: Open University Press, 1976). It was Locke (1632–1704) who popularized the terminology "primary and secondary qualities." But, as we shall see in Chapter 4, Locke's analysis of the distinction was not quite the same as Galileo's.

[4]Aristotle (384–322 B.C.) was the greatest scientist-philosopher of antiquity. His treatise on the basis of natural science is called *The Physics*. St. Thomas Aquinas (1225?–1274), the greatest philosopher-theologian of the Medieval Scholastic period (thirteenth and fourteenth centuries), had written a brilliant *Commentary on the Physics of Aristotle*.

[5]Francis Bacon (1561–1626) and Thomas Hobbes (1588–1679) should be mentioned in this connection, along with Galileo.

[6]Other arguments against direct realism are found in the "First Meditation" of Descartes, discussed in Chapter 1.

chapter 1

DESCARTES

THE FATHER OF MODERN PHILOSOPHY

A French Catholic of independent means and an independent turn of mind, René Descartes (1596–1650) was a most important figure in the avant-garde of modern thought. He was the first to work out a comprehensive natural science based on mechanistic and mathematical principles. He was the inventor of an indispensable tool of modern physics, analytic geometry. And he was called the Father of Modern Philosophy.

Descartes took it upon himself to construct, from "simple and indubitable" principles, a philosophical system hospitable to modern science (unlike Aristotelian philosophy) and at the same time inimical to atheistic materialism (unlike Democritus' philosophy). He wanted to justify the new physics and at the same time to set limits to it. The limits, he argued, are God and the mind of man. For God and the mind are not parts of physical nature and cannot be reduced to matter in motion. Physics is not metaphysics—reality includes more than material reality.

Descartes' masterpiece, and the great seminal work of modern philosophy, is the *Meditations on First Philosophy*, first published in 1641. ("First philosophy" means "metaphysics," the science of ultimate reality.) The *Meditations* are designed to deliver readers from uncritical reliance on the evidence of the senses and to lead them to a firm knowledge of the mind, of God, and of nature—a nature characterized by none but the primary qualities and knowable by way of mathematical reasoning.

Skepticism about the capacity of the human mind to attain knowledge of immaterial realities was on the rise in the seventeenth century. Descartes wanted to show that this skepticism grew from the same roots as skepticism about the mathematical methods of modern physics, namely uncritical reliance upon sense experience.

A careful study of the *Meditations* is the first major step toward an understanding of modern philosophy. As you study the six *Meditations* and the following analysis of them, try to think of objections and alternatives to what Descartes is saying. In so doing you may anticipate some of the ideas of the philosophers who succeeded him. For modern philosophy has been, to a large extent, the development of a series of more or less radical alternatives to the Cartesian system.

AN ANALYSIS OF THE MEDITATIONS

Meditation I: What Can be Called in Question?

Skeptics feel that we are all faced with a welter of conflicting opinions between which we have no adequate, objective means of choosing. (Montaigne: "Trying to know reality is like trying to clutch water.") They therefore recommend total suspension of judgment (*epoché*). Though not himself a committed skeptic (for he never gave up the search for Truth), Descartes does accept the skeptical *epoché* as a starting point for inquiry. Using arguments drawn from the ancient Greek skeptics, as well as one of his own invention (the "evil genius hypothesis"), he offers, as he tells us in his own "Synopsis of the Six Meditations,"

> reasons why we can doubt all things in general, and particularly, material objects, at least as long as we do not have other foundations for the sciences than those we have hitherto possessed.[1]

This general doubt, known as *methodic doubt,* serves as an instrument for removing the prejudices that stand in the way of constructing a truly solid foundation for science.

The major prejudice to be removed is the common opinion, shared by Aristotelian philosophers, that the source of our best and most certain knowledge is sense experience. Descartes argues as follows against this opinion, known as *empiricism*: A large object (the sun, for example) looks small at a distance. A bottle containing millions of minute objects (air particles) looks empty. Thus the senses sometimes deceive us, at least about remote or minute objects. But are there not other cases in which deception is impossible and doubt precluded? For example, the senses tell me that I am now sitting in a chair, holding a pen in my hand. Can I doubt this?—Yes, so long as I cannot exclude the possibility that I am *dreaming* these things:

> How often, in the still of the night, I have the familiar conviction that I am here, wearing a cloak, sitting by the fire—when really I am undressed and lying in bed! . . . I see so plainly that sleep and waking can never be distinguished by any certain signs, that I am bewildered. . . . (p. 62)[2]

The "argument from dreaming" has persuaded Descartes that his sense experiences may all be just so many pictures of ficticious or unreal scenes. But now he asks: Don't I at least have to admit that the *simple parts* or *elements* of these pictures stand for something real? Aren't the elements of even the most abstract compositions—lines, planes, volumes—drawn from reality? In order to bring even this very plausible belief into doubt, Descartes constructs the hypothesis of an almighty deceiver, "an evil genius who does his utmost to deceive me."

> How do I know he has not brought it about that, while in fact there is no earth, no sky, no extended objects, no shape, no size, no place, yet all these things should appear to exist as they do now? (pp. 63–64)

The issue is not whether this hypothesis is *plausible* (admittedly it isn't) but whether it is *possible* or *conceivable*. For if this universal deception is even possible, then we can never *know* that any of our representations (ideas and beliefs) are really true. For knowledge, certain knowledge, requires the removal of all possibility of error.

Meditation II: The Nature of the Human Mind: It is Better Known than the Body

Here Descartes begins to work his way out of total skepticism. He finds that he cannot doubt his own existence: If I doubted many things, I must exist! Even if the Great Deceiver is deceiving me, "then again I undoubtedly exist; let him deceive me as much as he may, he will never bring it about that, at the time of thinking that I am something, I am in fact nothing" (p. 67).[3]

"What am I?" At this point Descartes is certain of his existence only so far as he is a conscious thing (*res cogitans*); he is not yet certain of the real existence of his body, or indeed of any bodily (corporeal) thing.

First he defines "body," explaining that extension in length, breadth, and depth is what constitutes the very essence of corporeal substance. Accordingly, he refers to corporeal (bodily) substance as *res extensa*.

Having clarified the concept of body, Descartes still suspends judgment as to the real existence of bodies. At this point he admits only the existence of *res cogitans.* But suppose, he asks, "that these very things [bodies] which I suppose to be nonentities ... are yet in reality not different from the 'I' of which I am aware" (p. 69). Responding to his own question, he says: "I can judge only about the things I am aware of ... [and] this 'I' of which I am aware, ... precisely as such, does not depend on things of whose existence I am not yet aware ... " (pp. 69–70). He is saying that his *concept* of himself as a thinking thing is not understood or defined with reference to any bodily thing. Whether any thinking thing, as he defines it, can really *exist* apart from bodily substance, is a question he does not pretend conclusively to answer until a later stage (Meditation VI).

What is a conscious being? "A being that doubts, understands, asserts, denies, is willing, is unwilling; further, that has sense and imagination" (p. 70). The most certain knowledge that I have is knowledge of myself as a subject of conscious states and acts. Thus, for example, I may not be certain that there is really a typewriter in front of me; but I cannot help being sure that I am having certain experiences—that I *seem* to see something.

Descartes is here bringing out a characteristic feature of first person, present tense psychological statements, namely their *incorrigibility.* For example: If I tell you that there is a typewriter in front of us, you may correct me by saying that my statement is based on faulty observation (due to bad lighting, for example). But if I tell you that I *seem to see* a typewriter (or that I am *in pain,* or that I *intend* to do such and such), then it is not open to you to correct me in the same way.

The "piece of wax" passage: Here Descartes wants to break down any empiricist prejudice that the "common-sensical" reader might still retain. "I cannot help thinking," says the common-sense empiricist, "that corporeal objects, whose images are formed in consciousness are known far more distinctly than this 'I'"; he might give as a prime example of something distinctly known a piece of wax in front of him, something that he sees and touches. Descartes wants to show that, if we perceive the wax at all, it is not really perceived by the senses, or by the imaginative faculty (which stores past sense impressions), but only by the intellect.

If I put the wax by a fire, it loses its fragrance, the color changes, etc. Is the *same* wax, then, still there? If so, what was there in the wax that was so distinctly known? Nothing that I got through the senses; for whatever fell under taste, etc. has now changed.

If I remove what is not essential to the wax, what remains is something extended, flexible, and changeable. Now understanding that it's changeable does not consist in *imagining* the wax to be capable of many changes, for I comprehend its potentiality for an *infinity* of such changes, and yet I cannot run through an infinite number of them in my imagination. So I do not know the nature of the wax by imagination, but by purely mental perception.

In ordinary language we would speak of seeing the piece of wax. But in truth we do not *see* the wax at all; rather, we *judge or infer* from certain signs (including certain sensations) that the wax is present. It is by the purely mental power of judgment that we are aware of the wax. "When I distinguish the wax from its outward form, and as it were unclothe it and consider it in its naked self, I get something which . . . I need a human mind to perceive" (p. 74).

If I am to know about the reality of any physical object, it will be, then, through reason rather than sensation. Moreover, even if I am wrong in all my judgments about bodies, the existence of my mind is certain. For if I judge that the wax exists, it follows necessarily not that the wax exists, but that *I* exist.

Meditation III: God's Existence

Here Descartes tries to prove that, far from being the creature of some deceiving evil genius, he is really the creation of a supremely perfect Being who cannot be a deceiver.

His starting point is the contents of his own consciousness: *ideas* ("as it were pictures of objects," including sensations, images, and purely intellectual concepts), *acts of will and emotions,* and *judgments.*

Error is found not in ideas as such, nor in acts of will and emotion, but only in judgments. Error can arise only when I judge that an idea within myself has some similarity or conformity to some external object.

I have a natural impulse to judge that some of my ideas proceed from external objects. But can I be sure that nature is not deceiving me here? Is it possible that *all* of my ideas are constructions of my own mind, and that none of them represent a reality independent of my own mind? No. There is at least *one* idea that could not be dependent on my mind alone—the idea of a supremely perfect Being, of God.

The basic argument to God's existence contained in this Meditation is known as the *trademark argument* and can be set out in seven steps:

1. Everything has a cause. ("The principle of causality")
2. The cause must have at least as much reality as its effect. ("The principle of causal adequacy")
3. Every idea in the mind must have a cause, which has as much inherent reality as the idea has representative reality.[4] (The idea of a simple machine and the idea of an ingenious and complicated machine are equally ideas: they have the same "inherent reality." But they differ in "representative reality": *what* they represent is quite different. Now the idea of an ingenious machine represents something ingenious, and must therefore be due to a cause which is inherently ingenious—for example, an ingenious mechanic.)
4. I have the idea of an infinitely perfect Being.
5. Only an infinitely perfect Being has enough inherent reality to be the cause of the great representative reality contained in the idea of an infinitely perfect

being. (I, imperfect being that I am, certainly could not be responsible for the idea of such a supremely perfect Reality!)

6. That Being, God, must have implanted the idea of himself in me.
7. Therefore, God exists.

(It might of course be wondered whether the steps of this proof have the kind of self-evident truth Descartes claimed for them. Is there a premise that strikes you as particularly dubious? If so, why?)

God is no deceiver. For deceit depends on some defect, and a supremely perfect Being has no defect. Knowing this, I now have some right to confidence in the intelligibility of the world and in my ability to understand it. (Compare Einstein: "The good Lord is subtle but not malicious!")

Meditation IV: The Problem of Error

If I was created by a supremely perfect Being, why do I sometimes fall into error? Because I sometimes misuse my faculty of judgment. Although my mind is limited in its understanding, it is unlimited in its power of free will. And free will includes the power to abstain from believing what is not quite certain and thoroughly examined. I am directly conscious of this freedom within my own mind, and nothing can be more evident to me.

But why didn't God create me in such a way that I would never go wrong? God does innumerable things, the reasons for which no finite being can comprehend.

"For this very reason, I consider the usual enquiries about final causes to be wholly useless in physics; it could not but be rash, I think, for me to investigate the aims of God" (p. 94). Here Descartes is rejecting the teleological physics of Aristotle and the Middle Ages, which had explained natural processes by giving their "final causes" or purposes. (The Greek word *telos* means purpose or aim.) Descartes is saying that a teleological explanation of the natural world must go beyond any understanding that the human mind can hope to possess. Human physics must be content to explain *how* the planets move, for example; it cannot hope to explain *why* (for what purpose) they move as they do.

Meditation V: The Nature of Material Things; God's Existence again Considered

I find within myself ideas of objects that have their own real and unchangeable natures. For example, when I think of a triangle I see that there exists a certain determinate nature (triangularity, the essence or form of a triangle). Even if no triangles should actually exist in the material world, still this nature must be real. That it is no figment of my imagination and does not depend on my mind is implied by the fact that I can prove various properties of the triangle even if I have not thought of them when I previously imagined a triangle.

I have knowledge of the *essence* of material things by way of my ideas of extension, size, shape (including triangularity), position, and local motion. But this knowledge does not imply the actual *existence* of material things.

I have the idea of a supremely perfect Being (God). This is no fiction depending on my own way of thinking, but the image of a real and immutable nature.

My knowledge of this nature *does* imply actual existence. For I see that existence is part of the real and immutable nature signified by the word "God."

> God has all perfections.
> To exist is a perfection.
> Therefore, God exists.

(This is a version of what Immanuel Kant labeled "the ontological argument." It is a proof of the reality [Greek *on*] of something on the basis of its concept [*logos*] alone.)

Apart from knowledge of God, no perfect knowledge is possible. Since I now know that God exists and is perfectly good, I can be absolutely sure that I was not created so as to go wrong even about what appears to me most evident.

Meditation VI: The Existence of Material Things and the Real Distinction of Mind and Body

A. The existence of the material world and the proper use of the senses The real essence of material things must be definite and distinct, while my sensory apprehension of it is in many ways confused and obscure. Therefore I must not equate sensory apprehension with certain knowledge of the real essence of things. Such knowledge must consist in an apprehension of the primary qualities of matter—number, shape, size, etc. For they are the only material properties of which I can achieve a clear and distinct understanding. And I can achieve such an understanding only through the intellectual apprehension provided by mathematics, the science of number and quantity.

Although sense experience does not reveal the essence of the material world, it does—when supplemented with knowledge of God's goodness—reveal the *existence* of the material world. God created in me a very great natural inclination to believe that my sense experiences are caused in me by the action of material objects. If no such objects exist—if God hadn't bothered to create them—then he would be a deceiver, rather than the infinitely perfect Being that he is.

Since God is not deceitful, all of nature's lessons, even the obscure and confused apprehension of the senses, must contain *some* sort of truth. Thus nature teaches that I have a body and that it has an environment of other bodies, some of which must be shunned and others sought for. And, from the wide variety of colors, sounds, etc. of which I have sensations, I am right to infer that in the bodies from which these various sensations arise there is a corresponding, though perhaps not similar, variety.

Many other beliefs, which may seem to be lessons of nature, really derive from a habit of careless judgment—for example, the belief that a region is empty if no occurrence in it affects my senses, or the belief that if a body is hot, it has some property just like my idea of heat.

The proper function of sense experience is practical rather than theoretical in nature. It was given to me for the sole purpose of indicating to the mind what is good or bad for the whole, of which the mind is a part; to this extent it is clear enough. But if I use it as if it were a sure criterion for a direct judgment as to the essence of external objects, than it gives only very obscure and confused indications.

A new problem of error arises here about the objects that nature teaches us to seek or shun. For example, a sick person may have a great inclination to eat food that would be harmful to him. Why didn't God make us immune to such errors?

The solution is that, given God's decision to create us as a union of mind and body, there is no possibility that all such errors be precluded. The body is a machine, governed by mechanical laws. But the mind is a system of nonmechanical processes and is not, like the body, divisible into parts. The disparity between body and mind is such that no precise articulation between them is possible. Mind and body interact only in the brain, and so the mind's influence does not permeate the body. Thus the possibility of the mind's deception by its body is inevitable.[5]

God's goodness guarantees only that *statistically* we are not deceived by our sensations in matters important for health and action. "I know that all my sensations are much more often true than delusive signs in matters regarding the well-being of the body ... " (p. 124). And God has given me *memory*, by which I can learn from experience when not to trust my sensations.

I can now see a vast difference between waking experience and dreaming experience.

> Dreams are never connected by memory with all the other events of my life. ... If in waking life somebody suddenly appeared and directly afterwards disappeared, as happens in dreams, ... I should justifiably decide that he was a ghost, or a phantasm formed in my own brain, rather than a real man. But when I distinctly observe where an object comes from, where it is, and when

this happens; and when I can connect the perception of it uninterruptedly with the whole of the rest of my life, then I am quite certain that while this is happening to me I am not asleep but awake. And I need not doubt the reality of things at all, if after summoning all my senses, my memory, and my understanding to examine them, these sources yield no conflicting information. (p. 124)

B. The real distinction between mind and body My mind is tightly bound to my body: what happens in one causally influences what happens in the other. For example, there is usually a causal connection between my feelings of hunger and an emptiness of my stomach.

Although there happens to be interaction between them, mind and body remain really distinct. That is, it is logically possible for the one to exist without the other; in other words, God could keep the one in being separately from the other. God willed that hunger pangs are a sign of an empty stomach, but he could have willed otherwise. He could have given "hunger pangs" to a pure spirit—although that would have been mischievous of him and incompatible with his supreme goodness.

I have a clear and distinct idea of myself taken simply as a conscious, not an extended being. I have a distinct idea of body, taken simply as an extended, not a conscious being. Whatever I clearly and distinctly understand can be made by God just as I understand it. So, since I clearly understand my mind as something distinct from my body, God could have made the one without the other.

MAJOR ISSUES OF MODERN PHILOSOPHY

Descartes thought that he had arrived at a firm and fundamentally complete philosophy. Later philosophers did not agree. They valued his works more for the questions they brought into focus than for the answers they provided. Prominent among these questions are the following five:

1. *The Problem of Perception:* If things as they really are can be so different from things as they present themselves in human experience, then how can we ever hope to *know* anything about them? If physical things are not given to the mind directly, as objects of perception, then how can we ever be sure of their existence?

2. *The Empiricism/Rationalism Problem:* What is the role of the senses in relation to pure thought?

3. *The Freedom/Determinism Problem:* Is the conviction that our wills are free compatible with the axiom of physics and metaphysics, which says that everything is caused?

4. *The Mind/Body Problem:* Is our understanding of the mind really clear and distinct enough for us to be sure that it is an immaterial thing? And if it is immaterial, how can it possibly interact with the material body?

5.   *The Problem of Rational Theology:* What is the role and justification of belief in God? Are there any sound arguments for the existence of God?

It was Descartes' position on the mind/body problem that provoked the strongest and most immediate critical reactions—reactions vividly portrayed in the following imaginary dialogue between Princess Elizabeth of Bohemia and her philosophical mentor, René Descartes. Written by Godfrey Vesey of the Open University, it is based on letters exchanged by the princess and the philosopher in the 1640s.[6]

READING

THE PRINCESS
AND THE PHILOSOPHER[7]

[*Conversation and music in a large hall*]

DESCARTES   Madame, the honour that your Highness does in greeting me is greater than I dared to hope. It is most consoling not only to receive the favour of your commandments in writing, but to encounter you.

ELIZABETH   You are welcome, Master. Your letters have given me much pleasure.

DESCARTES   I am most obliged to your Highness for reading them. Even when you see how badly I explain myself, you still have patience to hear me. [*Slight pause*] But tell me, Madame, how can I help you and what subjects still bemuse your Highness? When I read the traces of your thought on paper, I find a truly amazing comprehension of the abstract matters on which I write. But now, seeing before me a body such as painters give to angels, from which these superhuman sentiments flow, I am ravished like a man come fresh to heaven. Anything you ask, I will answer, if I can.

ELIZABETH   Let us move to a quieter room.

[*They move to a quiet room and sit down*]

ELIZABETH   I wrote to you, you will remember, about the nature of the soul. I asked you how the soul, if it is an immaterial thing, can move the body. Surely, if one object is to move another, the first must be in physical contact with the second. I cannot play my harpsichord without touching the keys with my fingers. How can the soul, if it is purely spiritual, touch the body to bring about changes in it?

DESCARTES   Forgive me, Madame, I answered that question, did I not?

ELIZABETH   You replied to my letter, but I don't think you answered my question. You wrote that people suppose heaviness to be something that moves objects, and yet moves them without their being touched. Heaviness makes the leaves fall to the ground and this is obviously different from the way that one ball, when it strikes another, makes it move. In other words—and this I took to be your point—we do have a notion of one thing moving another without making contact with it.

DESCARTES   Ah ... so you agree with me.

ELIZABETH   [*Slight pause—continues puzzled*] But the way in which heaviness moves the leaves is very different from the way the soul moves the body. Heaviness is not immaterial in the way that, according to you, the soul is immaterial. It isn't—how shall I put it?—heaviness isn't a *mental* force. What I can't understand is how a thought can bring about a bodily movement. You aren't saying that it does so by heaviness, are you? In any case, I don't known what that means.

DESCARTES   No, no, no, no, no. My point is that we do have a notion of things being moved without other things making physical contact with them. [*Slight pause*] As a matter of fact, this notion is misapplied when we use it to understand why things fall to the ground. In my *Physics* I showed that the heaviness of things is not, in fact, something distinct from them. But we do have this notion and I believe we were given it in order to understand how the soul moves the body. If, by using this notion, we can understand how the soul moves the body, we can also see how a man's soul and body are united.

ELIZABETH   But all the emphasis, in your *Meditations,* is on their being distinct.

DESCARTES   Yes, but there are two things to remember about the soul. First, it is a thing which thinks. Second, it is united to the body, and so can act and suffer along with it. I said almost nothing about the second in my *Meditations*. My aim there was to show that the soul is distinct from the body, and it would only have confused matters to have said, at the same time, that they are united.

ELIZABETH   [*Interrupting*] Oh yes, but now you must explain. Because if you simply say that the soul and body are united, and leave it at that, I'm really no better off. How can what is spiritual be united with what is corporeal, physical, material, "extended"? Master, I accept that soul and body are united, but if I am to understand how the soul can act on the body, I must understand the principle of their union. How are soul and body, two distinct substances, united?

DESCARTES   [*Pensively*] Well, it isn't by the intellect, with which we comprehend the soul, that we can also understand the union of soul and body. Nor is it by the intellect aided by the imagination. That leaves only the senses. So it is through the senses that we understand the union of soul and body. When we philosophize on these matters we realize that soul and body are distinct; but so far as our experience is concerned it's as if they were one. When I raise my arm, or have a pain in my back, I don't feel myself to be separate from my arm or my back. But I know, nevertheless, that my soul is distinct from my body.

ELIZABETH   You are saying that it *feels* as if body and soul are united?

DESCARTES   Indeed.

ELIZABETH   But that doesn't explain *how* they are united, does it? You said we understand the union of soul and body by the senses. But knowing *that* the soul acts on the body isn't knowing how. [*Pause*] You see, it seems to me that if the soul and body do act on one another, then we ought to be able to understand how they do so. The senses don't seem to provide that sort of knowledge. [*Descartes still does not reply*] It was because I couldn't see how the immaterial soul could act on the physical body that I suggested that the soul, in its substance as distinct from its activity, must be material. If thinking, willing, and so on, are things that the *body* does, instead of things done by a spiritual thing which is distinct from the body, my problem doesn't arise.

DESCARTES   But what do you mean by "substance"? It's the soul's activities—thinking, willing, and so on—that make it the substance it is. Thought is the essence of the soul, just as "extension"—taking up space—is the essence of matter. No substance can have two essences.

ELIZABETH   [*Indignant*] Yet I clearly remember your saying in a letter that I could "ascribe matter and extension to the soul."

DESCARTES   When was that?

ELIZABETH   About three years ago, I think.

DESCARTES   In what connection?

ELIZABETH   I can find the letter for you. [*She rummages*] Yes, here it is. Let me find the place . . . Ah! "Your Highness remarks that it is easier to ascribe matter and extension to the soul than to ascribe to an *im*material thing the ability to move a material thing and be moved by it. Now I would ask your Highness to feel free to ascribe matter and extension to the soul . . . "

DESCARTES   Ah, but how does it go on?

ELIZABETH   Er" . . . matter and extension to the soul; for this is nothing else than to conceive the soul as united to the body."

DESCARTES   [*Animated*] You see! I was still talking about the soul being united to the body. The soul is, in a sense, extended. For example, when we feel aches and pains in various parts of our bodies. . . . Suppose you prick your finger on a spindle . . .

ELIZABETH   Aren't you confusing me with another Princess?

DESCARTES   I said "suppose." Suppose you prick your finger on a spindle. You feel pain. Where do you feel the pain? In your finger. In a way it's almost as if your soul were extended throughout your body, even into your fingers. But to talk in that way is to talk only of feeling. The pain isn't really in your finger, it's in your soul. You know by your intellect that it isn't in your finger, since you know by your intellect that the soul, which suffers pain, is immaterial. To know the truth of the matter we must trust the intellect.

ELIZABETH   The intellect, you say, tells us that the soul is immaterial. But is our intellectual perception of the soul sufficiently clear? Perhaps, if we had a clearer perception of its nature we would realize that it is, in fact, material. Isn't there at least this possibility?

DESCARTES   Not if the argument of my *Meditations* is sound. You remember, I imagined that an extremely powerful, malicious demon does everything he can to deceive us?

ELIZABETH   Yes.

DESCARTES   He may deceive me about everything that has to do with my body, but when it comes to my thinking—well, then he can't deceive me. That I cannot doubt. [*Slowly and emphatically*] Therefore, in so far as I cannot be deceived about my existence I am no more than a thinking thing.

ELIZABETH   Agreed. But that is "what you cannot be deceived about." The question I'm raising is a different one. It isn't about what you do or don't know; it's about what is in fact the case. I'm suggesting that although you can suppose yourself not to have bodily attributes it may nevertheless be the case that you do have them.

DESCARTES   No. They may seem quite different questions—the one about what I know or don't know and the one about what is in fact the case—but they aren't. They're connected.

ELIZABETH   How? How are they connected?

DESCARTES   Well, it's really to do with possibilities. If it is possible for thinking to go on apart from a body then . . .

ELIZABETH   [*Interrupting*] But *is* it possible? That's the question.

DESCARTES   All right, I'm coming to that. I did say "if." If it is possible for thinking, and the body, to exist in separation then . . .

ELIZABETH   [*Impatiently*] Yes, yes, then what-does-the-thinking isn't the body. I can quite see that. But what you've got to do is to get rid of the "if." That is, you've got to show it to be possible for thinking to go on apart from a body.

DESCARTES   Precisely, and that is where what I know and don't know, comes in.

ELIZABETH   Go on.

DESCARTES   Well, I know certainly that I am thinking and at the same time I can doubt that I have bodily attributes. So I can perceive the one thing, the thinking, apart from the other. And since this perception is clear and distinct it must be possible for the one thing to exist apart from the other.

ELIZABETH   Just a moment. You said "since this perception is clear and distinct."

DESCARTES   Yes.

ELIZABETH   And you'd say that if you clearly and distinctly perceive yourself as no more than a thinking thing then it would follow that you could exist as no more than a thinking thing?

DESCARTES   Yes.

ELIZABETH   And therefore that you really are no more than a thinking thing?

DESCARTES   Exactly.

ELIZABETH   All right. Well now, isn't it possible that your perception is clear, but only as far as it goes? And that it doesn't go far enough for you to know the truth? In other words, isn't it possible that you really do have bodily properties although your knowledge of yourself doesn't go beyond your mental properties.

DESCARTES   No. You must distinguish between clearness and completeness. Certainly there may be things about me which I haven't clearly perceived. But that doesn't affect what I have clearly perceived. And, having clearly perceived that I am a thinking thing, I know that I can exist as such. That is, I know that what I am certain of—my intellectual faculty—is enough for me to exist with. And if it is enough for me to exist with, then I really am distinct from anything bodily.

ELIZABETH   So, the principle of your argument is: if I can clearly perceive something to be such-and-such while I cannot clearly perceive it to be so-and-so, then it can exist simply as such-and-such.

DESCARTES   Yes.

ELIZABETH   But now, consider this case. A triangle is a plane figure bounded by three straight lines.

DESCARTES   Mm.

ELIZABETH   That is something most people know. But not everyone knows that the angles of a triangle add up to two right angles. That is, someone might know very well that something was a triangle, and yet not know this further fact about its angles. Now, on your reasoning it should be possible for there to be a triangle whose angles did not add up to two right angles. Do you see what I mean?

DESCARTES   Yes, it's the same point as Father Arnauld made in the fourth set of objections to my *Meditations*. But I do not accept that they are parallel cases. And I say why in my answer to him.

ELIZABETH   I'll have to look at that again. [*Pause*] You see, it isn't that I don't want to believe you. Unless you are right about the soul being distinct from the body, I don't see how there can be any hope of life after death. If it is some part of my body that thinks and wills, then when it decays in death there is an end of me. On your view, moreover, God has made in his likeness. Only if we perceive ourselves to be purely spiritual can we think of God likewise. These thoughts are precious to me, Master Descartes. I accept them as a matter of faith, but I would that faith and reason should go together. [*Sighs*] The soul grows weary of its burdensome shroud of flesh. There are times when I long to be released from it to a happier life above.

DESCARTES   Madame, I know of the exile that threatens you, and I grieve that there is nothing I can do to help.

ELIZABETH   But there is, Master Descartes. There is. Your letters are a great comfort to me and I hope you'll continue to write. Thus shall the months seem weeks, and the weeks days.

DESCARTES   I wish I could be of more material service to you. I wish . . .

ELIZABETH   [*Interrupting*] Go now, good master. Go out and make free of the court which has banished me. Turn their hearts and minds to philosophy as you have turned mine. It is their evil that I must bear. Moderate it if you can . . .

FOR FURTHER READING

ELIZABETH ANSCOMBE and PETER GEACH, trans. and ed., *Descartes' Philosophical Writings*. Indianapolis: Bobbs-Merrill, 1971. Contains an outstanding translation of important, selected texts. Especially recommended, along with the *Meditations,* are the first four Parts of the *Discourse* and the selections from the *Principles of Philosophy*.

ELIZABETH S. HALDANE and G.R.T. ROSS, trans., *The Philosophical Works of Descartes*. Cambridge, England: Cambridge University Press, 1911. Volume II contains sets of objections from Descartes' contemporaries, and Descartes' replies to them.

JOHN COTTINGHAM, *Descartes*. Oxford: Blackwell, 1986. A probing, yet sympathetic and accessible exposition of the whole range of Descartes' thought.

ALEXANDER SESONSKE and NOEL FLEMING, eds., *Meta-Meditations*. Belmont, Calif.: Wadsworth, 1966. A useful collection of critical and interpretative articles on Descartes.

O. K. BOUWSMA, "Descartes' Evil Genius," *The Philosophical Review*, LVIII (Jan., 1949). An entertaining but profound critique of Descartes' use of the appearance-reality distinction. (Reprinted in Sesonske and Fleming.)

E.M. CURLEY, *Descartes Against the Skeptics*. Cambridge, Mass.: Harvard University Press, 1978.

EZRA TALMOR, *Descartes and Hume*. New York: Pergamon, 1980. Contains useful information on Descartes vis-à-vis the Scholastics.

nature in which we live and have our being. Therefore Spinoza saw it as the expression of an unhealthy way of life and a false ethic.

The *Ethics* has five Parts:

I   Of God
II   On the Nature and Origin of the Mind
III On the Origin and Nature of the Affects
IV   Of Human Bondage, Or of the Strength of the Affects
V   Of the Power of the Intellect, or of Human Liberty

e will be trying to understand some of the main concepts in the first two rts. A full discussion of Spinoza's lengthy and difficult masterpiece would far beyond the scope of this introductory book.

VACUUM ARGUMENT

ntral idea of the *Ethics*, the notion of the underlying oneness or unity ings, can be seen as developing out of the following argument from es' *Principles of Philosophy:*

impossibility of a vacuum in the philosophical sense—a place in which e is absolutely no substance—is obvious from the fact that the extension space or intrinsic place is in no way different from the extension of a For the extension of a body in length, breadth and depth justifies us in ding that it is a substance, since it is wholly contradictory that there be extension that is the extension of nothing; and we must draw the onclusion about the supposedly empty space, viz. that since there is on there, there must necessarily be substance there as well. (II.XVI, be & Geach trans., p. 205)

athan Bennett is responsible for stressing the significance of for an understanding of Spinoza; the following exposition is Section 24 of his recent commentary, *A Study of Spinoza's*

all the air out of a jar, what is left in it?—There cannot be eft, for if there were nothing between the two sides they ous. We might try to get out of this by saying that there is its sides. To this Descartes replies that distance is a or quality or measure—and there must be something it a mile of road or a yard of fabric, but you cannot have aked yard. The moral is that the jar must still contain l: it may lack mass, solidity, impenetrability, etc., but it th size and shape—not a nothing with size and shape. rguing against the existence of a vacuum in the ordi-

---

GODFREY VESEY, ed., *Philosophy in the Open.* Milton Keynes, England: The Open University Press, 1974. Contains much illuminating material on problems of modern philosophy.

QUESTIONS

1. If something very strange happens or seems to happen to us, we may wonder if we're dreaming. We may then pinch ourselves to make sure that we are really awake. What would Descartes say about this?

2. How would Descartes respond to the following argument? "I know that physical objects (shoes, ships, sealing wax, etc.) exist because I can see and touch them!" Do *you* consider this is a satisfactory argument?

3. Why is "I am thinking" indubitable in a way in which, say, "I am sweating" is not?

4. What objection would Descartes make to behaviorism (the view that all knowledge of psychological states is derived from observation of behavior)? (Review the analysis of Meditation Two.)

5. Give the gist of the trademark argument in your own words, then explain your reactions to it. Do you think it proves the existence of God?

6. An old objection to the *Meditations* accuses its author of circular reasoning:

> Descartes claims to prove the trustworthiness of the intellect by demonstrating that it is the workmanship of a good creator, God. But before he can take such a "proof" seriously, he must *already* be convinced that his intellect is trustworthy.

Do you think that this objection is based on a fair interpretation of the *Meditations*? (Can you find texts that seem to provoke the "circularity objection"?) Also, consult the following: Anscombe and Geach, eds., *Descartes' Philosophical Writings,* p. 184, and Haldane and Ross, *The Philosophical Works of Descartes,* Vol. II, pp. 38–43. Based on these texts, how would Descartes respond to the "circularity objection"?

7. What do you think of the "ontological argument"? What, in particular, do you think of the premise, "Existence is a perfection"?

8. In the *Discourse on Method,* Part IV, Descartes presents the following argument for the distinction between mind and body:

> I cannot doubt that I exist.
> I can doubt that any physical thing exists.
> Therefore, I am not a physical thing.

If you grant that the two premises are true, are you forced to admit the truth of the conclusion?

9. Starting with Galileo, most modern philosophers maintained that "hot" names a sensation that we feel, rather than a quality in things. Descartes formulated the following argument in order to prove Galileo's point:

> I have a sensation of heat as I approach the fire; but when I approach the same fire too closely, I have a sensation of pain; so there is nothing to convince me that something in the fire resembles heat, any more

than the pain; it is just that there must be something in it (whatever this may turn out to be) that produces the sensations of heat or pain. (Sixth Meditation, pp. 118–119 in Anscombe and Geach).

Analyze this argument. What is its conclusion? What are the premises? Is any premise dubious? Does the conclusion follow from the premises?

10.   What is "representational realism" and how did Descartes try to prove it? (Review the preceding Introduction, as well as Descartes' Sixth Meditation.) Do you think his proof is sound?

11.   The human being, according to Descartes, is a union of two essentially different but causally interacting things. This position, known alternatively as *dualistic interactionism* or *Cartesian dualism,* is developed and defended in Meditations Two and Six. Review that material and then explain, first, what led Descartes to insist on the *duality* of mind and body (the possibility of their independent existence) and, second, what led him to speak of an *interaction* between mind and body. Finally, summarize and assess what The Princess had to say in objection to her mentor's position.

NOTES

[1]Descartes, *Meditations on First Philosophy,* Lawrence J. Lafleur, trans. (Indianapolis: Bobbs-Merrill, 1960), p. 13.

[2]This, and all quotations to follow, are from the outstanding translation by Elizabeth Anscombe and Peter Geach, *Descartes: Philosophical Writings* (Indianapolis: Bobbs-Merrill, 1971). All page references are to that volume. Reprinted with permission of Macmillan Publishing Co., copyright © 1971.

[3]In his earlier work, the *Discourse on Method* (Part Four), Descartes expressed this insight in the now-famous words, *Cogito ergo sum* ("I think, therefore I am").

[4]What Anscombe and Geach translate as "inherent" and "representative reality," others translate as "formal" and "objective reality."

[5]I am indebted to Elizabeth Anscombe for the material in this paragraph.

[6]See Anscombe and Geach, ed. and trans., *Descartes: Philosophical Writings,* pp. 274–286. See also Antoine Arnauld's objections to the *Meditations* in Haldane and Ross, trans., *The Philosophical Works of Descartes* (New York: Cambridge University Press, 1955), Vol. II, pp. 83–85, and Descartes' reply to Arnauld on pp. 100–102 of the same volume.

As Professor Vesey acknowledges, the use of the geometrical example towards the end of his dialogue comes not from the Descartes–Elizabeth correspondence, but from Arnauld's objections.

[7]From Chapter 6 of *Philosophy in the Open* (Milton Keynes, England: Open University Press, 1974), edited by Godfrey Vesey. Reprinted with permission of the publisher.

chapter 2

SPINOZA

THE PROPHET OF THE ONENESS OF ALL

Baruch Spinoza was born into the Jewish
and excommunicated from it for his h
changed his name to its Latin equiv
had heard the ancient call, "Hear, O
eronomy 6:4). His heresy consisted
kind: all things are One" (or wor

The greatest influence on
ing, was the philosophy of Re
orthodox Cartesian any more
Descartes saw thought and ex
ing substances, Spinoza can
same substance.

Spinoza's fame as
published in 1677, the y
the ethical one of poi
he concluded, that is
between the mind a
this union, encourag

nary sense of that term, i.e., "region of extension which does not have mass." He is arguing against "vacuum" in the sense of "extended nothing." His point is that what we ordinarily call empty space, because it contains nothing perceptible to the senses, is actually something real. An "empty" space is just a particularly thin region of a single reality: *res extensa*, extended substance. There is only one extended substance: space.

This idea was taken over and developed by Spinoza. According to Spinoza, all physical objects are so many qualities ("modes") of one substance, namely the whole of space. Regions of space get various qualities, such as impenetrability, mass, etc., so that any statement asserting the existence of a physical object reduces to one saying something about a region of space. What, in everyday speech, we refer to as things in space are really intermittent thickenings *of* space. The difference between matter and empty space, ordinarily so called, is just the difference between thick and thin regions of space. And so everything that we say about material reality reduces to statements about a single ultimate subject or substance.

Now it was Descartes' position that, although there is only one material reality—extended substance, or space—there are many spiritual realities—many thinking substances. Spinoza's radical break with Descartes came with his rejection of this sort of mind/matter dualism. Spinoza argued that there is only *one* thinking substance, and that it is identical with material substance. But before we can see how Spinoza developed this idea, we must understand some of the technical terms employed in the *Ethics*, namely the distinction between *substance* and *mode* and the notion of an *attribute*.

SUBSTANCE, MODES, AND ATTRIBUTES

The term substance (*ousia*) has been used since the time of Aristotle to signify "that which exists in itself," i.e., "a thing, as opposed to a quality, state, 'accident' or 'mode'." On this definition, a tree, for example, would be a substance, while the color and shape of the tree would be qualities or modes of the tree. But on Spinoza's modified definition, a tree would not *really* be a substance, for by *substance* he means "that which is [exists] in itself and is conceived through itself; that is, that the conception of which does not require the conception of another thing from which it is to be formed" (*Ethics* 1d3).[2] A tree is really a *mode:* "that which is in something else and is conceived through something else" (1d5). A tree exists in space and is conceived, or explained, in terms of the laws governing spatial reality, i.e., the laws of physics.

For Spinoza, nature is the totality of modes, that is, the sum total of all the qualities and states of substance. Now a mode is knowable only in terms of an *attribute*, an attribute being "that which the intellect perceives of substance as constituting its essence" (1d4).

MIND AND BODY

As noted before, Spinoza includes not only qualities (hardness, etc.) but also what we ordinarily call things (trees, etc.) under the heading *modes*. We must now emphasize that he includes not only physical things and qualities under that term but also mental, or psychological things and qualities—that is, minds, and mental predicates such as thought and feeling. But, unlike Descartes, Spinoza does not conclude that there must be two different sorts of substances, one (*res extensa*) to support physical predicates and another (*res cogitans*) to support the psychological. His position is, rather, that extension and thought are two attributes of one and the same underlying reality. His position is, to spell it out further, that *all* modes (everything in nature) fall under *both* attributes; that, in other words, each modification of extended substance is identical with some mode of thinking substance, and vice versa. For example, there is a mode X, which the intellect perceives under the attribute "thought" as a *pain,* but under the attribute "extension" as a *brain state.* There is one reality, X, which can be understood in two ways: either in the psychological language of sensations or in the physical language of brain states. Physics and psychology give us two different, and irreducible, ways of understanding one and the same sequence of natural events.

PANPSYCHISM

The thesis that *all* extended things are also thinking things is a form of *panpsychism,* the view that everything has a soul (Greek *psychē*). It sounds strange to speak of a tree (for example) as a thinking thing, but perhaps less so once we know that Spinoza uses the term "thinking" so broadly that it includes "subconscious desires and perceptions" as well as conscious ones. Thus he is not committed to saying that trees and molecules have a conscious mental life, as do man and other higher animals.

Panpsychism is opposed to the theory that mental states have somehow evolved out of wholly nonmental antecedents. For it holds that only antecedents that are already in some degree mental could cause or explain mental effects. In other words (using Spinoza's terminology): Thought and extension are two *basic* and *irreducible* attributes of reality, therefore you cannot explain a fact about something's mental properties by reference to physical causes. Therefore we must reject the materialist view according to which mind has evolved out of unthinking substance.

Descartes viewed man as essentially different from everything else in nature; for man alone, he thought, had a mind or soul, and therefore a certain freedom from the system of mechanical causes and effects which constituted the rest of nature. To use Spinoza's image, Descartes saw man as "a kingdom within a kingdom," whereas Spinoza saw him as "a little whirlpool within a big flood" (to borrow an image from Jonathan Bennett). For Spinoza, the mind of man differs in degree but not in kind from the rest of nature.

DEUS, SIVE NATURA

Naturalism is the metaphysical theory that says that nature is a self-existing, self-regulating, and homogeneous[3] system. Spinoza subscribed to this theory and combined it with another—*pantheism*. Pantheism is the form of naturalism that says that nature is *God,* where "God" means the infinite, unitary, and self-existent cause of all existence.

Spinoza accepted Descartes' proofs for the existence of God. But he denied that Descartes was entitled to draw a theistic conclusion from them. *Theism* is the metaphysical theory that says that God (the infinite, unitary, self-existent cause of all things) is a personal being who created nature out of nothing and directs it according to teleological laws.

In spite of his "methodic doubt," Descartes held onto many beliefs inherited from the Middle Ages, theism among them. Spinoza's rejection of theism stamped him as the more radically modern thinker.

Reality equals *substance and all its modes; substance and all its modes* equals *God, or nature (Deus, sive Natura).* Using these equations, Spinoza tried to transfer the religious attitude of worshipful awe and humble love from "God, the personal Creator of nature" to "God, the impersonal system of nature itself."

Spinoza's *nature* is a *deterministic system,* which means that every event taking place within it is caused by another, antecedent, event within the system. Since, in such a system, every event is explained in terms of antecedent causes, there can be no legitimate appeal to final causes. For to say that an event occurred because of some end ("in order to produce a future event") is incompatible with saying that the event is part of a deterministic system (where everything happens because of a past, antecedent, event).

READING

FROM THE ETHICS[4]

As the major reading for this chapter, I have chosen the Appendix to Part One of the Ethics, *a spirited essay in which Spinoza summarizes his own (naturalistic) theology and then attacks traditional (theistic) theology, along with the teleological conception of nature implied by it. This reading is preceded by a few pages from the beginning of the Ethics, material which illustrates the geometrical style characteristic of the work.*

PART 1: CONCERNING GOD

Definitions

1. By that which is self-caused I mean that whose essence involves existence; or that whose nature can be conceived only as existing.
2. A thing is said to be finite in its own kind (*in suo genere finita*) when it can be limited by another thing of the same nature. For example, a body is said to be finite because we can always conceive of another body greater than it. So, too, a thought is limited by another thought. But body is not limited by thought, nor thought by body.
3. By substance I mean that which is in itself and is conceived through itself; that is, that the conception of which does not require the conception of another thing from which it has to be formed.
4. By attribute I mean that which the intellect perceives of substance as constituting its essence.
5. By mode I mean the affections of substance; that is, that which is in something else and is conceived through something else.
6. By God I mean an absolutely infinite being; that is, substance consisting of infinite attributes, each of which expresses eternal and infinite essence.

Explication   I say 'absolutely infinite,' not 'infinite in its kind.' For if a thing is only infinite in its kind, one may deny that it has infinite attributes. But if a thing is absolutely infinite, whatever expresses essence and does not involve any negation belongs to its essence.

7. That is said to be free (*liber*) which exists solely from the necessity of its own nature, and is determined to action by itself alone. A thing is said to be necessary (*necessarius*) or rather, constrained (*coactus*), if it is determined by another thing to exist and to act in a definite and determinate way.
8. By eternity I mean existence itself insofar as it is conceived as necessarily following solely from the definition of an eternal thing.

Explication   For such existence is conceived as an eternal truth, just as is the essence of the thing, and therefore cannot be explicated through duration or time, even if duration be conceived as without beginning and end.

Axioms

1. All things that are, are either in themselves or in something else.
2. That which cannot be conceived through another thing must be conceived through itself.
3. From a given determinate cause there necessarily follows an effect; on the

other hand, if there be no determinate cause it is impossible that an effect should follow.

4. The knowledge of an effect depends on, and involves, the knowledge of the cause.

5. Things which have nothing in common with each other cannot be understood through each other; that is, the conception of the one does not involve the conception of the other.

6. A true idea must agree with that of which it is the idea (*ideatum*).

7. If a thing can be conceived as not existing, its essence does not involve existence.

Proposition 1

Substance is by nature prior to its affections.

Proof   This is evident from Defs. 3 and 5.

Proposition 2

Two substances having different attributes have nothing in common.

Proof   This too is evident from Def. 3; for each substance must be in itself and be conceived through itself; that is, the conception of the one does not involve the conception of the other.

Proposition 3

When things have nothing in common, one cannot be the cause of the other.

Proof   If things have nothing in common, then (Ax.5) they cannot be understood through one another, and so (Ax.4) one cannot be the cause of the other.

Proposition 4

Two or more distinct things are distinguished from one another either by the difference of the attributes of the substances or by the difference of the affections of the substances.

Proof   All things that are, are either in themselves or in something else (Ax.1); that is, (Defs. 3 and 5), nothing exists external to the intellect except substances and their affections. Therefore there can be nothing external to the intellect through which several things can be distinguished from one another except substances or (which is the same thing) (Def. 4) the attributes and the affections of substances.

Proposition 5

In the universe there cannot be two or more substances of the same nature or attribute.

Proof   If there were several such distinct substances, they would have to be distinguished from one another either by a difference of attributes or by a difference of affections (Pr.4). If they are distinguished only by a difference of attributes, then it will be granted that there cannot be more than one substance of the same attribute. But if they are distinguished by a difference of affections, then, since substance is by nature prior to its affections (Pr.1), disregarding therefore its affections and considering substance in itself, that is (Def. 3 and Ax.6) considering it truly, it cannot be conceived as distinguishable from another substance. That is (Pr.4), there cannot be several such substances but only one.

Proposition 6

One substance cannot be produced by another substance.

Proof   In the universe there cannot be two substances of the same attribute (Pr.5), that is (Pr.2) two substances having something in common. And so (Pr.3) one cannot be the cause of the other; that is, one cannot be produced by the other.

Corollary   Hence it follows that substance cannot be produced by anything else. For in the universe there exists nothing but substances and their affections, as is evident from Ax.1 and Defs. 3 and 5. But, Pr.6, it cannot be produced by another substance. Therefore substance cannot be produced by anything else whatsover.

Another Proof   This can be proved even more readily by the absurdity of the contradictory. For if substance could be produced by something else, the knowledge of substance would have to depend on the knowledge of its cause (Ax.4), and so (Def.3) it would not be substance.

Proposition 7

Existence belongs to the nature of substance.

Proof   Substance cannot be produced by anything else (Cor.Pr.6) and is therefore self-caused (*causa sui*); that is (Def.1), its essence necessarily involves existence; that is, existence belongs to its nature.

• • •

APPENDIX

I have now explained the nature and properties of God: that he necessarily exists, that he is one alone, that he is and acts solely from the necessity of his own nature, that he is the free cause of all things and how so, that all things are in God and are so dependent on him that they can neither be nor be conceived without him, and lastly, that all things have been predetermined by God, not from his free will or absolute pleasure, but from the absolute nature of God, his infinite power. Furthermore, whenever the opportunity arose I have striven to remove prejudices that might hinder the apprehension of my proofs. But since there still remain a considerable number of prejudices, which have been, and still are, an obstacle—indeed, a very great obstacle—to the acceptance of the concatenation of things in the manner which I have expounded, I have thought it proper at this point to bring these prejudices before the bar of reason.

Now all the prejudices which I intend to mention here turn on this one point, the widespread belief among men that all things in Nature are like themselves in acting with an end in view. Indeed, they hold it as certain that God himself directs everything to a fixed end; for they say that God has made everything for man's sake and has made man so that he should worship God. So this is the first point I shall consider, seeking the reason why most people are victims of this prejudice and why all are so naturally disposed to accept it. Secondly, I shall demonstrate its falsity; and lastly I shall show how it has been the source of misconceptions about good and bad, right and wrong, praise and blame, order and confusion, beauty and ugliness, and the like.

However, it is not appropriate here to demonstrate the origin of these misconceptions from the nature of the human mind. It will suffice at this point if I take as my basis what must be universally admitted, that all men are born ignorant of the causes of things, that they all have a desire to seek their own advantage, a desire of which they are conscious. From this it follows, firstly, that men believe that they are free, precisely because they are conscious of their volitions and desires; yet concerning the causes that have determined them to desire and will they do not think, not even dream about, because they are ignorant of them. Secondly, men act always with an end in view, to wit, the advantage that they seek. Hence it happens that they are always looking only for the final causes of things done, and are satisfied when they find them, having, of course, no reason for further doubt. But if they fail to discover them from some external source, they have no recourse but to turn to themselves, and to reflect on what ends would normally determine them to similar actions, and so they necessarily judge other minds by their own. Further, since they find within themselves and outside themselves a considerable number of means very convenient for the pursuit of their own advantage—as, for instance, eyes for seeing, teeth for chewing, cereals and living creatures for food, the sun for giving light, the sea for breeding fish—the result is that they look on all the things of Nature as means to their own advantage. And realising that these were found, not produced by them, they come to believe that there is someone else who produced these means for their use. For looking on things as means, they could not believe them to be self-created, but on the analogy of the means which they are accustomed to produce for themselves, they were bound to conclude that there was some governor or governors of Nature, endowed with human freedom, who have attended to all their needs and made everything for their use. And having no information on the subject, they also had to esti- mate the character of these rulers by their own, and so they asserted that the gods direct everything for man's use so that they may bind men to them and be held in the highest honour by them. So it came about that every individual devised different methods of worshiping God as he thought fit in order that God should love him beyond others and direct the whole of Nature so as to serve his blind cupidity and insatiable greed. Thus it was that this misconception developed into superstition and became deep-rooted in the minds of men, and it was for this reason that every man strove most earnestly to understand and to explain the final causes of all things. But in seeking to show that Nature does nothing in vain—that is, nothing that is not to man's advantage—they seem to have shown only this, that Nature and the gods are as crazy as mankind.

Consider, I pray, what has been the upshot. Among so many of Na- ture's blessings they were bound to discover quite a number of disasters, such as storms, earthquakes, diseases and so forth, and they maintained that these occurred because the gods were angry at the wrongs done to them by men, or the faults committed in the course of their worship. And although daily experience cried out against this and showed by any number of exam- ples that blessings and disasters befall the godly and the ungodly alike with- out discrimination, they did not on that account abandon their ingrained prejudice. For they found it easier to regard this fact as one among other mysteries they could not understand and thus maintain their innate condi- tion of ignorance rather than to demolish in its entirety the theory they had constructed and devise a new one. Hence they made it axiomatic that the judgment of the gods is far beyond man's understanding. Indeed, it is for this reason, and this reason only, that truth might have evaded mankind forever had not Mathematics, which is concerned not with ends but only with essences and properties of figures, revealed to men a different stan- dard of truth. And there are other causes too—there is no need to mention them here—which could have made men aware of these widespread miscon- ceptions and brought them to a true knowledge of things.

I have thus sufficiently dealt with my first point. There is no need to spend time in going on to show that Nature has no fixed goal and that all final causes are but figments of the human imagination. For I think that this is now quite evident, both from the basic causes from which I have traced the origin of this misconception and from Proposition 16 and the Corollaries to Proposition 32, and in addition from the whole set of proofs I have adduced to show that all things in Nature proceed from an eternal necessity and with supreme perfection. But I will make this additional point, that this doctrine of Final Causes turns Nature completely upside down, for it regards as an effect that which is in fact a cause, and vice versa. Again, it makes that which is by nature first to be last; and finally, that which is highest and most perfect is held to be the most imperfect. Omitting the first two points as self-evident, Propositions 21, 22 and 23 make it clear that that effect is most perfect which is directly produced by God, and an effect is the less perfect in proportion to the number of intermediary causes required for its production. But if the things produced directly by God were brought about to enable him to attain an end, then of necessity the last things for the sake of which the earlier things were brought about would excel all others. Again, this doctrine negates God's perfection; for if God acts with an end in view, he must necessarily be seeking something that he lacks. And although theologians and metaphysicians may draw a distinction between a purpose arising from want and an assimilative purpose, they still admit that God has acted in all things for the sake of himself, and not for the sake of the things to be created. For prior to creation they are not able to point to anything but God as a purpose for God's action. Thus they have to admit that God lacked and desired those things for the procurement of which he willed to create the means—as is self-evident.

I must not fail to mention here that the advocates of this doctrine, eager to display their talent in assigning purpose to things, have introduced a new style of argument to prove their doctrine, i.e. a reduction, not to the impossible, but to ignorance, thus revealing the lack of any other argument in its favour. For example, if a stone falls from the roof on somebody's head and kills him, by this method of arguing they will prove that the stone fell in order to kill the man; for if it had not fallen for this purpose by the will of God, how could so many circumstances (and there are often many coinciding circumstances) have chanced to concur? Perhaps you will reply that the event occurred because the wind was blowing and the man was walking that way. But they will persist in asking why the wind blew at that time and why the man was walking that way at that very time. If you again reply that the wind sprang up at that time because on the previous day the sea had begun to toss after a period of calm and that the man had been invited by a friend, they will again persist—for there is no end to questions—"But why did the sea toss, and why was the man invited for that time?" And so they will go on and on asking the causes of causes, until you take refuge in the will of God—that is, the sanctuary of ignorance. Similarly, when they consider the structure of the human body, they are astonished, and being ignorant of the causes of such skilful work they conclude that it is fashioned not by mechanical art but by divine or supernatural art, and is so arranged that no one part shall injure another.

As a result, he who seeks the true causes of miracles and is eager to understand the works of Nature as a scholar, and not just to gape at them like a fool, is universally considered an impious heretic and denounced by those to whom the common people bow down as interpreters of Nature and the gods. For these people know that the dispelling of ignorance would entail the disappearance of that astonishment, which is the one and only support for their argument and for the safeguarding their authority. But I will leave this subject and proceed to the third point that I proposed to deal with.

When men become convinced that everything that is created is created on their behalf, they were bound to consider as the most important quality in every individual thing that which was most useful to them, and to regard as of the highest excellence all those things by which they were most bene-fited. Hence they came to form these abstract notions to explain the natures of things:—Good, Bad, Order, Confusion, Hot, Cold, Beauty, Ugliness; and since they believed that they are free, the following abstract notions came into being:—Praise, Blame, Right, Wrong. The latter I shall deal with later on after I have treated of human nature; at this point I shall briefly explain the former.

All that conduces to well-being and to the worship of God they call Good, and the contrary, Bad. And since those who do not understand the nature of things, but only imagine things, make no affirmative judgments about things themselves and mistake their imagination for intellect, they are firmly convinced that there is order in things, ignorant as they are of things and of their own nature. For when things are in such arrangement that, being presented to us through our senses, we can readily picture them and thus readily remember them, we say that they are well arranged; if the contrary, we say that they are ill-arranged, or confused. And since those things we can readily picture we find pleasing compared with other things, men prefer order to confusion, as though order were something in Nature other than what is relative to our imagination. And they say that God has created all things in an orderly way, without realising that they are thus attributing human imagination to God—unless perchance they mean that God, out of consideration for the human imagination, arranged all things in the way that men could most easily imagine. And perhaps they will find no obstacle in the fact that there are any number of things that far surpass our imagination, and a considerable number that confuse the imagination because of its weakness.

But I have devoted enough time to this. Other notions, too, are noth-ing but modes of imagining whereby the imagination is affected in various ways, and yet the ignorant consider them as important attributes of things because they believe—as I have said—that all things were made on their behalf, and they call a thing's nature good or bad, healthy or rotten and corrupt, according to its effect on them. For instance, if the motion communicated to our nervous system by objects presented through our eyes is conducive to our feeling of well-being, the objects which are its cause are said to be beautiful, while the objects which provoke a contrary motion are called ugly. Those things that we sense through the nose are called fragrant or fetid, through the tongue sweet or bitter, tasty or tasteless, those that we sense by touch are called hard or soft, rough and smooth, and so on. Finally, those that we sense through our ears are said to give forth noise, sound, or harmony, the last of which has driven men to such madness that they used to believe that even God delights in harmony. There are philosophers who have convinced themselves that the motions of the heavens give rise to harmony. All this goes to show that everyone's judgment is a function of the disposition of his brain, or rather, that he mistakes for reality the way his imagination is affected. Hence it is no wonder—as we should note in passing—that we find so many controversies arising among men, resulting finally in scepticism. For although human bodies agree in many respects, there are very many differences, and so one man thinks good what another thinks bad; what to one man is well-ordered, to another is confused; what to one is pleasing, to another is displeasing, and so forth. I say no more here because this is not the place to treat at length of this subject, and also because all are well acquainted with it from experience. Everybody knows those sayings:—"So many heads, so many opinions," "everyone is wise in his own sight," "brains differ as much as palates," all of which show clearly that men's judgment is a function of the disposition of the brain, and they are guided by imagination rather than intellect. For if men understood things, all that I have put forward would be found, if not attractive at any rate convincing, as Mathematics attests.

We see therefore that all the notions whereby the common people are wont to explain Nature are merely modes of imagining, and denote not the nature of any thing but only the constitution of the imagination. And because these notions have names as if they were the names of entities existing independently of the imagination I call them 'entities of imagination' (*entia imaginationis*) rather than 'entities of reason' (*entia rationis*). So all arguments drawn from such notions against me can be easily refuted. For many are wont to argue on the following lines: if everything has followed from the necessity of God's most perfect nature, why does Nature display so many imperfections, such as rottenness to the point of putridity, nauseating ugliness, confusion, evil, sin, and so on? But, as I have just pointed out, they are easily refuted. For the perfection of things should be measured solely from their own nature and power; nor are things more or less perfect to the extent that they please or offend human senses, serve or oppose human interests. As to those who ask why God did not create man in such a way that they should be governed solely by reason, I make only this reply, that he lacked not material for creating all things from the highest to the lowest degree of perfection; or, to speak more accurately, the laws of his nature were so comprehensive as to suffice for the production of everything that can be conceived by an infinite intellect, as I proved in Proposition 16.

These are misconceptions which I undertook to deal with at this point. Any other misconception of this kind can be corrected by everyone with a little reflection.

FOR FURTHER READING

JOHN WILD, ed., *Spinoza Selections*. New York: Scribner's, 1930. I recommend Wild's Introduction.

BARUCH SPINOZA, *The Ethics and Selected Letters*, translated by Samuel Shirley. Indianapolis: Hackett, 1982. The beginner is advised to spend more time on the Propositions and Appendices than on the Proofs.

BARUCH SPINOZA, *Theological-Political Treatise*, in *Works of Spinoza*, translated by R.H. Elwes. New York: Dover, 1955. This fascinating work contains an early defense of freedom of religion along with an interesting interpretation of the Bible.

ISAAC BASHEVIS SINGER, "The Spinoza of Market Street," in *The Spinoza of Market Street and Other Stories*. New York: Avon Books, 1963. A vivid picture of someone who lives by Spinozistic philosophy.

STUART HAMPSHIRE, *Spinoza*. Baltimore: Penguin, 1962. The outstanding elementary introduction.

JONATHAN BENNETT, *A Study of Spinoza's "Ethics."* Indianapolis: Hackett, 1984. Advanced and rigorous, but clearly written. This whole chapter is much indebted to it.

PAUL WIENPAHL, *The Radical Spinoza*. New York: New York University Press, 1979. Presents a somewhat mystical interpretation of Spinoza. An interesting contrast with Bennett.

QUESTIONS

1. Summarize and evaluate Descartes' "vacuum argument," and relate it to Spinoza's system.

2. *Define:* substance, mode, attribute, mind, matter, panpsychism.

3. The panpsychist, it might be objected, applies psychological terms such as "thought" and "desire" so broadly that they come to lose their meaning. What do you think of this objection? Do you think that Descartes would have been sympathetic to it? Explain.

4. What is Spinoza's theory of the relationship between mind and body? Do you think it represents an improvement over Descartes'? Does it reply convincingly to the kind of questions posed by The Princess?

5. *Define:* naturalism, pantheism, theism, deterministic system, teleology.

6. The Scholastics, discussed in the Introduction, said that God is the *efficient* and the *final* cause of nature. What would Spinoza say?

7. Spinoza has been called a dangerous atheist, on the one hand, and a God-intoxicated man, on the other. Can you think of reasons in support of both views?

8. How does Spinoza account for the origin of the opinion that things in nature act with an end in view? (In Book II, Chapter 2 of his *Physics,* Aristotle had argued that nature acts purposively. You might want to compare his account with that of Spinoza.)

9. Discuss Spinoza's account of the origin of the idea of human free will and of the ideas of goodness and beauty.

10. Read Singer's "The Spinoza of Market Street" and sum up what it conveys about the Spinozistic way of life and view of reality. Do you think it contains an implicit criticism of that way of life and view of reality?

NOTES

[1]This phrase comes from *On the Improvement of the Understanding,* a kind of preparatory study for the *Ethics.* See John Wild, ed., *Spinoza Selections* (New York: Scribner's, 1930), p. 5.

[2]1d3 = Part I, Definition 3. The *Ethics,* written in the form of Euclid's *Elements of Geometry,* has definitions, axioms, propositions, demonstrations, corollaries, lemmas, scholia, and appendices.

[3]A homogeneous system is one whose parts differ in degree but not in kind. See the preceding paragraph.

[4]Baruch Spinoza, *The Ethics and Selected Letters,* trans. Samual Shirley, ed. Seymour Feldman (Indianapolis: Hackett Publishing Co., Inc., 1982), pp. 31–34, 57–62. Reprinted with the permission of the publisher.

chapter 3

LEIBNIZ

A DIPLOMAT AMONG PHILOSOPHERS

Mathematician and philosopher Gottfried Wilhelm von Leibniz (1646–1716) is best remembered for his invention of the calculus[1] and his philosophy of "the best of all possible worlds."

He was also a diplomat who applied his considerable diplomatic skills to the service of philosophy, as well as to the service of government.[2] Successful diplomats reconcile opposing parties. In philosophy, Leibniz tried to reconcile two apparently contradictory conceptions of nature: the mechanistic conception of Galilean physics and the teleological conception of scholastic philosophy.

You will learn the details of Leibniz's reconciling project from your study of the *Monadology*, the reading for this chapter. But to smooth the way for that, I provide the following overview of Leibnizian philosophy, which shows it in relation to the philosophies of Descartes and Spinoza.

OVERVIEW OF LEIBNIZ'S PHILOSOPHY

1. *Like Descartes and Spinoza, Leibniz was a rationalist. That is, he stressed the inadequacy of sense experience as a basis for knowing reality:*

> We use the external senses as . . . a blind man does a stick, and they make us know their particular objects, which are colors, sounds, odors, flavors, and the qualities of touch. But they do not make us know what these sensible qualities are or in what they consist.
>
> *Being* itself and *truth* are not known wholly through the senses; for it would not be impossible for a creature to have long and orderly dreams, resembling our *life,* of such a sort that everything which it thought it perceived through the senses would be but mere *appearances.* There must therefore be something beyond the senses, which distinguishes the true from the apparent.[3]

This "something beyond the senses" is *pure reason,* the faculty by which we grasp clear and distinct intelligible objects, including the criteria of being and truth.

2. *Unlike Descartes and Spinoza, Leibniz, was an idealist: He denied the reality of material substance.*

a) First he disposed of Descartes' argument for the reality of material substance as follows:

> The core of [Descartes'] argument is this: The reason for our sensation of material things is outide of us; therefore these sensations come to us either from God, or from some other agent, or from the things themselves. They do not come from God, if these things do not exist; for otherwise God would be a deceiver; they do not come from another agent—this he forgot to prove; therefore they come from he things themselves, which therefore must exist. It may be answered that the sensations may come from an agent other than God; for just as, for some weighty reason, he permits other evils, he may also permit this deceit, without thereby becoming a deceiver; the more so since this deception does not entail any damage to us. . . . Moreover, our souls may have deserved because of former sins to be condemned to this life full of deceptions, in which they take shadows for things. . . . [4]

b) Second, Leibniz formulated a positive theory of his own to replace the realist theory of Descartes and Spinoza, according to which material objects are qualities or states of one extended or spatial substance. For Leibniz, space and the whole extended world are merely the appearance of an underlying unextended reality: the system of *monads.* A monad is an indivisible center of perception and appetition—rather like a Cartesian *res cogitans.* The real world (a world visible not to the senses but to reason alone) is a hierarchy of these monads. The ones near the top of the hierarchy are very bright and sensitive, while the ones near the bottom are dull-witted and short on memory.

Material objects have no extra-mental reality, being nothing but certain coherent sets of ideas in the monads. Sense perception is nothing but a perfectly consistent dream. And physics, as the search for patterns in this "dream," must not pretend to inform us about the ultimate nature of reality.

Modern physics (Galilean mechanics) is nothing but mathematical analysis of this "perfectly consistent dream." It tells us about the mechanical (deterministic) laws governing nature *as it appears to us in senses experience*. But it tells us nothing of nature as a hierarchy of monads governed by teleological laws. Only pure (nonsensuous) reason can perceive the underlying reality of nature.

3. *Like Descartes and unlike Spinoza, Leibniz left room for contingency.*

a) If Spinoza was right about the identity of God with the world, then God could not have created a world different from the one that actually exists, for God is eternal and the eternal could not be other than it is. But it is obvious (Leibniz thought) that the actual world is one of many possible worlds. Therefore Spinoza was wrong.

b) According to Leibniz, any adequate philosophy must allow for a distinction between necessary truths ("truths of reason") and contingent truths ("truths of fact"). Leibniz drew the distinction in this way: *Necessary truths* are true of every possible world. They include the proposition of logic and mathematics, and all other propositions that cannot be denied without contradiction. *Contingent truths* are true only for the world that actually exists; had God chosen to create a different world, they would not all apply to it. For example, the propositions of zoology, inasmuch as they imply the existence of animals, would not be true of a world in which no animals exist. Contingent truths can be denied without contradiction.

If, as Leibniz thought, all propositions are fundamentally of the form "S is P" (where some subject is judged to have a certain characteristic or predicate), then we can say that in a necessary truth the predicate is contained in the essence (or definition) of the subject, while in a contingent truth the predicate is not contained in the essence of the subject.

4. *Like both Descartes and Spinoza, Leibniz accepted the ontological argument.*

An *existential proposition* asserts or implies the existence of something. Only one existential proposition is necessarily true: *God exists*. For "God" is the name of that being which is the source of all existence, and the source of all existence must contain within itself the sufficient reason of its own existence. God exists because his essence contains existence.

5. *Unlike Spinoza or Descartes, Leibniz held that nature is a teleological system, explainable in terms of final causality.*

a) Nature is the actually existing world. The actually existing world is one of many possible worlds. So there must be sufficient reason why God chose to make *it* exist, rather than some other possible world.

Since God is infinitely perfect, he always makes the best possible choices. Therefore, God created the actually existing world because it is the *best of all possible worlds*.

b) Spinoza's view was that nature is the *only* possible world. It exists out of an inner necessity, not from the choice of a supernatural creator. For Spinoza, neither "choice" nor "best" nor any teleological concept plays a role in true explanations of the nature of things.

c) Descartes would have to deny that there is but *one* actually existing world. For he viewed the human mind as a sort of world unto itself—something really distinct from the rest of nature. A mind was an unextended substance governed by teleological laws, while the rest of nature was an extended substance governed by mechanistic laws. The difficulty, of course, was to explain how these *two* worlds could be parts of *one* nature. This difficulty—the so-called mind/body problem—led post-Cartesian philosophers such as Spinoza and Leibniz to reject the dualism which had given rise to it.

READING

THE MONADOLOGY[5]

1. The monad, of which we shall here speak, is merely a simple substance entering into those which are compound; simple, that is to say, without parts.
2. And there must be simple substances, since there are compounds; for the compound is only a collection or aggregation of simple things.
3. Where there are no parts, neither extension nor figure, nor divisibility is possible; and these monads are the true atoms of nature and, in a word, the elements of things.
4. There is thus no danger of dissolution, and there is no conceivable way in which a simple substance can perish naturally.
5. For the same reason, there is no way in which a simple substance can begin naturally, since it could not be formed by composition.
6. Therefore we may say that the monads can neither begin nor end in any other way than all at once; that is to say, they cannot begin except by creation, nor end except by annihilation; whereas that which is compounded, begins and ends by parts.
7. There is also no intelligible way in which a monad can be altered or changed in its interior by any other created thing; since it would be impossible to transpose anything in it, or conceive in it any internal movements which could be excited, directed, augmented or diminished within, such as may take place in compound bodies, where there is change of parts. The monads have no windows through which anything can enter or go out. It would be impossible for any accidents [forms, qualities] to detach themselves and go forth from the substances, as did formerly the "sensible species"[6] of the Schoolmen [Scholastics]. Accordingly, neither substance nor accident can enter a monad from without.
8. Nevertheless monads must have qualities, otherwise they would not even be entities. And if simple substances did not differ in their qualities, there would be no means by which we could become aware of the changes of things, since all that is in compound bodies is derived from simple ingredients, and monads, if they were without qualities, would be indistinguishable one from another, since they do not differ in quantity. . . .

9. Moreover, each monad must differ from every other, for there are never two beings in nature perfectly alike, and in which it is impossible to find an internal difference, or one founded on some intrinsic denomination.

10. I assume furthermore, that every created being, and consequently the created monad, is subject to change; and likewise that this change is continual in each.

11. It follows, from what we have now said, that the natural changes of monads proceed from an internal principle, since no external cause can influence their interior.

12. But, besides the principle of change, there must also be a detail of that which changes, which constitutes, so to speak, the specific nature and the variety of the simple substances.

13. This detail must involve multiplicity in the unit or in that which is simple. For, as all natural changes proceed by degrees, something changes and something remains unchanged, and consequently there must be in the simple substance a plurality of affections and relations, although there are no parts.

14. This shifting state, which involves and represents multiplicity in the unit, or in the simple substance, is nothing but what we call *perception,* which must be carefully distinguished from *apperception,* or consciousness, as will appear in the sequel. Here it is that the Cartesians have especially failed, making no account of those perceptions of which we are not conscious. It is this that has led them to suppose that spirits are the only monads, and that there are no souls of brutes.... It is owing to this that they have vulgarly confounded protracted torpor with actual death, and have fallen in with the scholastic prejudice, which believes in souls entirely separate [from bodies]. For this reason, also, ill-affected minds have been confirmed in the opinion that the soul is mortal.

15. The action of the internal principle which causes the change, or the passage from one perception to another, may be called appetition. It is true, the desire cannot always completely attain to every perception to which it tends, but it always attains to something thereof, and arrives at new perceptions.

16. We experience in ourselves the fact of a multiplicity in the simple substance, when we find that the least thought of which we are conscious includes a variety in its object. Accordingly, all who admit that the soul is a simple substance, are bound to admit this multiplicity in the monad....

17. Besides, it must be confessed that perception and its consequences are inexplicable by mechanical causes, that is to say, by figures and motions. If we imagine a machine so constructed as to produce thought, sensation and perception, we may conceive it as magnified—the same proportions being preserved—to such an extent that one might enter it like a mill. This being supposed, we should find in it on inspection only pieces which impel each other, but nothing which can explain a perception. It is in the simple substance, therefore, and not in a compound, or in a machine, that we must look for the phenomenon of perception. And in the simple substance we find nothing else—nothing, that is, but perceptions and their changes. Therein also, and therein only, consist all the internal actions of simple substances.

18. We might give the name of *entelechies*[7] to all simple substances or created monads, inasmuch as there is in them a certain completeness (perfection). There is a certain sufficiency which makes them the sources of their own internal actions, and, as it were, incorporeal automata.

19. If we choose to give the name of soul to everything that has perceptions and desires, in the general sense which I have just explained, then all simple sub-

stances or created monads may be called souls. But as feeling is something more than simple perception, I am willing that the general name of monads or entelechies shall suffice for those simple substances which have perception only, and that the term souls shall be confined to those in which perceptions are more distinct, and accompanied by memory.

20. For we experience in ourselves a state in which we remember nothing, and have no distinct perception; as when we are in a swoon or in a profound or dreamless sleep. In this state the soul does not differ perceptibly from a simple monad; but since this state is not permanent, and since the soul delivers itself from it, the soul is something more. . . .

21. And it does not by any means follow, in that case, that the simple substance is without perception. That, indeed, is impossible, for the reasons given above; for it cannot perish, neither can it subsist without affection of some kind, which is nothing else than its perception. But where there is a great number of minute perceptions, and where nothing is distinct, one is stunned; as when we turn round and round in continual succession in the same direction, whence arises a vertigo, which may cause us to faint, and which prevents us from distinguishing anything. And possibly death may produce this state for a time in animals.

22. And as every present condition of a simple substance is a natural consequence of its antecedent condition, so its present is big [pregnant] with its future.

23. Then, as on waking from a state of stupor, we become conscious of our perceptions, we must have perceptions, although unconscious of them, immediately before awaking. For each perception can have no other natural origin but an antecedent perception, as every motion must be derived from one which preceded it.

24. Thus it appears that if there were no distinction—no relief, so to speak—no enhanced flavor in our perceptions, we should continue forever in a state of stupor; and this is the condition of the naked monad.

25. And so we see that nature has given to animals enhanced perceptions, by the care which she has taken to furnish them with organs which collect many rays of light and many undulations of air, increasing their efficacy by their union. There is something approaching to this in odor, in taste, in touch, and perhaps in a multitude of other senses of which we have no knowledge. I shall presently explain how that which passes in the soul represents that which takes place in the organs.

26. Memory gives to the soul a kind of *consecutiveness* which resembles reason, but must be distinguished from it. We observe that animals, having a perception of something which strikes them, and of which they have previously had a similar perception, expect, through the representation of their memory, the recurrence of that which was associated with it in their previous perception, and incline to the same feelings which they then had. For example, when we show dogs the cane, they remember the pain which it caused them, and whine and run.

27. And the lively imagination, which affects and excites them, arises either from the magnitude or the number of their previous perceptions. For often a powerful impression produces suddenly the effect of long *habit,* or of moderate perceptions often repeated.

28. In men as in brutes, the consecutiveness of their perceptions is due to the principle of memory—like empirical physicians, who practice without theory. Indeed we are mere empirics [empiricists] in three-fourths of our acts. For

example, when we expect that the sun will rise tomorrow, we judge so empirically, because it has always risen hitherto. It is only the astronomer who judges by an act of reason.

29. But the knowledge of necessary and eternal truths is what distinguishes us from mere animals. It is this which gives us *reason* and the sciences, and raises us to the knowledge of ourselves and of God; and it is this in us which we call a reasonable soul or *spirit.*

30. It is also by the knowledge of necessary truths, and by their abstractions, that we rise to *acts of reflection,* which give us the idea of that which calls itself "*I*', and which led us to consider that this or that is within *us.* And thus, while thinking of ourselves, we think of being, of substance, simple or compound, of the immaterial, and of God himself. We conceive that that which in us is limited, is in him without limit. And these reflective acts furnish the principal objects of our reasonings.

31. Our reasonings are founded on two great principles, that of *contradiction,* by virtue of which we judge that to be *false* which involves contradiction, and that to be *true* which is opposed to, or which contradicts the false.

32. And that of *sufficient reason,* by virtue of which we judge that no fact can be real or existent, no statement true, unless there be a sufficient reason why it is thus, and not otherwise, although these reasons very often cannot be known to us.

33. There are also two kinds of *truths,*—those of *reason* and those of *fact.* Truths of reason are necessary, and their opposite is impossible; those of fact are contingent, and their opposite is possible. When a truth is necessary, we may discover the reason of it by analysis, resolving it into simpler ideas and truths, until we arrive at those which are primitive.

34. It is thus that mathematicians by analysis reduce speculative *theorems* and practical *canons* to *definitions, axioms,* and *postulates.*

35. And finally, there are simple ideas of which no definition can be given; there are also axioms and postulates, in a word, *ultimate principles,* which cannot and need not be proved. And these are *identical propositions,* the opposite of which contains an express contradiction.

36. But there must also be a *sufficient reason* for *contingent truths,* or *truths of fact,* that is, for the series of things diffused through the universe of created objects, or else the process of resolving into particular reasons might run into a detail without bounds, on account of the immense variety of things in nature, and the infinite division of bodies. There is an infinity of figures and of movements, present and past, which enter into the efficient cause of my present writing; and there is an infinity of minute inclinations and dispositions of my soul, present and past, which enter into the final cause of it.

37. And as all this *detail* only involves other anterior or more detailed contingencies, each one of which again requires a similar analysis in order to account for it, we have made no advance; and the sufficient or final reason must be outside of the *series* of this detail of contingencies, however infinite this series may be.

38. And thus the final reason of things must be found in a necessary substance, in which the detail of changes exists only eminently, as in their source. And this substance we call *God.*

39. Now this substance being a sufficient reason of all this detail, which also is everywhere linked together, *there is only one God, and this God suffices.*

40. We may also conclude that this supreme substance, which is unique, universal, and necessary ... must be incapable of limits, and must contain as much of reality as is possible.

41. Whence it follows that God is perfect, *perfection* being nothing but the magnitude of positive reality taken exactly, setting aside the limits or bounds in that which is limited. And where there are no bounds (that is to say, in God), perfection is absolutely infinite.

42. It follows also that the creatures have their perfections from the influence of God, but they have their imperfections from their own nature, which is incapable of existing without limits. For it is by this that they are distinguished from God....

43. It is true, moreover, that God is not only the source of existences, but also of essences, so far as real, or of that which is real in the possible. For the divine understanding is the region of eternal truths, or of the ideas on which they depend, and without him there would be nothing real in the possibilities of things, and not only nothing existing, but also nothing possible.

44. At the same time, if there be a reality in the essences or possibilities, or in the eternal truths, this reality must be founded in something existing and actual, consequently in the existence of the necessary Being, in whom essence includes existence, or with whom it is sufficient to be possible in order to be actual.

45. Thus God alone (or the necessary Being) possesses this privilege, that He must exist, if He is possible; and since nothing can hinder the possibility of that which includes no limits, no negation, and consequently no contradictions, that alone is sufficient to establish the existence of God *a priori* [independent of experience]. We have likewise proved it by the reality of eternal truths. But we have also just proved it *a posteriori* [from an experienced effect] by showing that, since contingent beings exist, they can have their ultimate and sufficient reason only in some necessary Being, who contains the reason of his existence in himself.

46. Nevertheless, we must not suppose ... that eternal truths, being dependent upon God, are arbitrary, and depend upon his will, as Descartes ... appears to have held. This is true only of contingent truths, the principle of which is *fitness,* or the choice of the best; whereas necessary truths depend solely on his understanding, and are its inner object.

47. Thus God alone is the primitive unity, or the original simple substance of which all the created or derived monads are the products; and they are generated so to speak, by continual fulgurations [flashes, sparks] of the Divinity, from moment to moment, bounded by the receptivity of the creature, of whose existence limitation is an essential condition.

48. In God is *power,* which is the source of all; also *knowledge,* which contains the detail of ideas; and, finally, *will,* which generates changes or products according to the principle of optimism. And this corresponds to what, in created monads, constitutes the subject or the basis, [namely] the perceptive and the appetitive faculty. But in God these attributes are absolutely infinite or perfect; and in the created monads ... they are only imitations according to the measure of their perfection.

49. The creature is said to *act* externally, in so far as it possesses perfection, and to *suffer* from another [creature] in so far as it is imperfect. Thus we ascribe *action* to the monad, in so far as it has distinct perceptions, and *passivity,* in so far as its perceptions are confused.

50. And one creature is more perfect than another, in this, that we find in it that which serves to account *a priori* for what takes place in the other; and it is therefore said to act upon the other.

51. But in simple substances this is merely an *ideal* influence of one monad upon another, and it can have its effect only by the intervention of God, inasmuch as in the ideas of God any monad has a right to demand that God, in regulating the rest from the commencement of things, should have regard to it. For since a created monad can have no physical influence on the interior of another, it is only by this means that one can be dependent on another.

52. And hence it is that actions and passions in creatures are mutual. For God, comparing two simple substances, finds reasons in each which oblige him to adapt the one to the other. Consequently that which is *active* in one view, is passive in another; active in so far as what we clearly discern in it serves to account for that which takes place in another, and *passive* in so far as the reason of that which passes in it is found in that which is clearly discerned in another.

53. Now, as in the ideas of God there is an infinity of possible worlds, and as only one can exist, there must be a sufficient reason for the choice of God, which determines him to decide upon one rather than another.

54. And this reason can be no other than *fitness*, derived from the different degrees of perfection which these worlds contain, since each possible world has a claim to exist according to the measure of perfection which it enfolds.

55. And this is the cause of the existence of that Best, which the wisdom of God discerns, his goodness chooses, and his power effects.

56. And this *connection*, or this adaptation of all created things to each, and of each to all, implies in each simple substance relations which express all the rest. Each, accordingly, is a living and perpetual mirror of the universe.

57. And as the same city viewed from different sides appears quite different, and is *perspectively* multiplied, so, in the infinite number of simple substances, there are given, as it were, so many different worlds, which nevertheless, are only the perspectives of a single one, according to the different points of view of each monad.

58. And this is the way to obtain the greatest possible variety, along with the greatest possible order; that is to say, it is the way to obtain the greatest possible perfection.

59. Thus this hypothesis (which I may venture to pronounce demonstrated) is the only one which properly exhibits the greatness of God. . . .

60. We see, moreover, in what I have just stated, the *a priori* reasons why things could not be other than they are. For God, in ordering the whole, has respect to each part, and specifically to each monad, whose nature being to represent, is by nothing restrained from representing the whole of things; although, it is true, that this representation must needs be confused, as it regards the detail of the whole universe, and can be distinct only in relation to a small part of things, that is, in relation to those which are nearest, or whose relations to any given monad are greatest. Otherwise each monad would be a divinity. The monads are limited, not in the object, but in the mode of their knowledge of the object. They all tend confusedly toward the infinite, toward the whole; but they are limited and distinguished by the degrees of distinctness in their perceptions.

61. And compounds symbolize in this respect simple substances. For since the world is a *plenum* [fullness], and all matter connected, and as in a *plenum* every

movement has some effect on distant bodies, in proportion to their distance, so that each body is affected not only by those in actual contact with it, and feels in some way all that happens to them, but also through their means is affected by others in contact with those by which it is immediately touched— it follows that this intercommunication extends to any distance however great. Consequently, each body feels all that passes in the universe, so that he who sees all, may read in each that which passes everywhere else, and even that which has been and shall be, discerning in the present that which is removed in time as well as in space. . . . But each soul can read in itself only that which is distinctly represented in it. It cannot unfold its laws at once, for they reach into the infinite.

62. Thus, though every created monad represents the entire universe, it represents more distinctly the particular body to which it belongs, and whose entelechy[8] it is; and as this body expresses the entire universe, through the connection of all matter in a *plenum,* the soul represents also the entire universe in representing that body which especially belongs to it.

63. The body belonging to a monad, which is its entelechy or soul, constitutes, with its entelechy, what may be termed a *living being,* and, with its soul, what may be called an *animal.* Now this body of a living being, or of an animal, is always organic; for every monad, being a mirror of the universe, according to its fashion, and the universe being arranged with perfect order, there must be the same order in the representative, that is, in the perceptions of the soul, and consequently in the body, through which the universe is represented in it.

64. Thus each organic living body is a kind of divine machine, or a natural automaton, infinitely surpassing all artificial automata. A machine made by human art is not a machine in all its parts. For example, the tooth of a brass wheel has parts or fragments which are not artificial to us, and which have nothing to mark the machine in relation to the use for which the wheel is designed. But nature's machines, that is, living bodies, are still machines in their minutest parts, *ad infinitum* [to infinity]. This constitutes the difference between nature and art, that is to say, between the divine art and ours.

65. And the Author of Nature has been able to exercise this divine and infinitely wonderful art, inasmuch as every portion of nature is not only infinitely divisible, as the ancients knew, but is actually subdivided without end, each part into parts, of which each has its own movement. Otherwise, it would be impossible that each portion of matter should express the universe.

66. Whence it appears that there is a world of creatures, of living beings, of animals, of entelechies, of souls, in the minutest portion of matter.

67. Every particle of matter may be conceived as a garden of plants, or as a pond full of fishes. But each branch of each plant, each member of each animal, each drop of their humors, is in turn another such garden or pond.

68. And although the earth and the air embraced between the plants in the garden, or the water between the fishes of the pond, are not themselves plant or fish, they nevertheless contain such, but mostly too minute for our perception.

69. Thus there is no uncultivated spot, no barrenness, no death in the universe, no chaos, no confusion, except in appearance, somewhat as it might appear in a pond at a distance, in which one would see a confused movement and swarming, so to speak, of the fishes of the pond, without separately distinguishing the fishes themselves.

70. We see, then, that each living body has a governing entelechy, which in animals is the soul of the animal. But the members of this living body are full of other living beings—plants, animals—each of which has its entelechy, or regent [ruling] soul.

71. We must not, however, suppose, as some who misapprehend my thought have done, that each soul has a mass or portion of matter proper to itself, or forever united to it, and that it consequently possesses other inferior living beings, destined forever to its service. For all bodies are in a perpetual flux, like rivers. Their particles are continually coming and going.

72. Thus the soul does not change its body except by degrees. It is never deprived all at once of all its organs. There are often metamorphoses in animals, but never metempsychosis, i.e., transmigration of souls. Neither are there souls entirely separated [from bodies], nor genii without bodies. God alone is wholly without body.

73. For which reason, also, there is never complete generation nor complete death—strictly considered—consisting in the separation of the soul from the body. That which we call *generation,* is development and accretion; and that which we call *death,* is envelopment and diminution.

74. Philosophers have been much troubled about the origin of forms, of entelechies, or souls. But at the present day, when, by accurate investigations of plants, insects and animals, they have become aware that the organic bodies of nature are never produced from chaos or from putrefaction, but always from a seed, in which undoubtedly, there had been some *preformation,* it has been inferred that not only the organic body existed in that seed before conception, but also a soul in that body, in one word, the animal itself; and that, by the act of conception, this animal is merely disposed to a greater transformation, in order to become an animal of another species. We even see something approaching this, outside of generation, as when worms become flies, or when caterpillars become butterflies.

75. Those *animals,* of which some are advanced to a higher grade by means of conception, may be called *spermatic;* but those among them which remain in their kind, that is to say, the greater portion, are born, multiply, and are destroyed, like the larger animals, and only a small number of the elect among them pass to a greater theater.

76. But this is only half the truth. I have concluded that if the animal does not begin to be in the order of nature, it also does not cease to be in the order of nature; and that not only there is no generation, but no entire destruction, or death, strictly speaking. And these *a posteriori* conclusions, drawn from experience, accord perfectly with my principles deduced *a priori,* as stated above.

77. Thus we may say not only that the soul (mirror of an indestructible universe) is indestructible but also the animal itself, although its machine may often perish in part. . . .

78. These principles have furnished me with a natural explanation of the union, or rather the conformity between the soul and the organized body. The soul follows its proper laws, and the body likewise follows those which are proper to it, and they meet in virtue of the *pre-established harmony* which exists between all substances, as representations of one and the same universe.

79. Souls act according to the laws of final causes, by appetitions, means and ends; bodies act according to the laws of efficient causes, or the laws of motion. And the two kingdoms, that of efficient causes and that of final causes, are in harmony with one another.

80. Descartes recognized that souls communicate no force to bodies, because the quantity of force in matter is always the same. Nevertheless, he believed that souls might change the direction of bodies. But this was because the world was at that time ignorant of the law of nature, which requires the conservation of the same total direction in matter. Had he known this, he would have hit upon my system of pre-established harmony.

81. According to this system, bodies act as if (to suppose the impossible) there were no souls, and souls act as if there were no bodies; and yet both act as though the one influenced the other.

• • •

83. Among other differences which exist between *spirits* and ordinary souls, some of which have already been indicated, there is also this: that souls in general are living mirrors, or images of the universe of creatures, but spirits are, furthermore, images of Divinity itself, or of the Author of Nature, capable of knowing the system of the universe, and of imitating something of it by architectonic examples, each spirit being, as it were, a little divinity in its own department.

84. Hence spirits are able to enter into a kind of fellowship with God. In their view he is not merely what an inventor is to his machine (which is the relation of God to other creatures), but also what a prince is to his subjects, and even what a father is to his children.

85. Whence it is easy to conclude that the assembly of all spirits must constitute the City of God, that is to say, the most perfect state that is possible, under the most perfect of monarchs.

86. This City of God, this truly universal monarchy, is a moral world within the natural; and it is the most exalted and the most divine among the works of God. It is in this that the glory of God most truly consists, for it would be wanting if his greatness and his goodness were not recognized and admired by spirits. It is in relation to this Divine City that he possesses, properly speaking, the attribute of goodness, whereas his wisdom and his power are everywhere manifest.

87. As we have established above a perfect harmony between the two natural kingdoms,—the one of efficient, the other of final causes,—it behooves us to notice here also still another harmony between the physical kingdom of nature and the moral kingdom of grace, that is to say, between God considered as the architect of the mechanism of the universe, and God considered as monarch of the divine City of Spirits.

88. This harmony makes all things conduce to grace by natural methods. This globe, for example, must be destroyed and repaired by natural means, at such seasons as the government of spirits may require, for the chastisement of some and recompense of others.

89. We may say, furthermore, that God as architect satisfies entirely God as legislator, and that accordingly, sins must carry their punishment with them in the order of nature, and by virtue even of the mechanical structure of things; and that good deeds in like manner will bring their recompense, through their connection with bodies, although this cannot, and ought not always to happen immediately.

90. Finally, under this perfect government, there will be no good deed without its recompense, and no evil deed without its punishment. And all must redound to the advantage of the good, that is to say, of those who ... confide in Providence after having done their duty, and who worthily love and imitate

the Author of all good, pleasing themselves with the contemplating of his perfections, following the nature of genuine *pure love,* which makes us happy in the happiness of the beloved. In this spirit the wise and good labor for that which appears to be conformable to the divine will, . . . recognizing that if we were sufficiently acquainted with the order of the universe we should find that it surpasses all the wishes of the wisest, and that it could not be made better than it is, not only for all in general, but for ourselves in particular, if we are attached, as is fitting, to the Author of All, . . . who alone can make us blest.

FOR FURTHER READING

PHILIP P. WIENER, ed., *Leibniz Selections.* New York: Scribner's, 1951.
L. J. RUSSELL, "Leibniz, Gottfried Wilhelm," in *The Encyclopedia of Philosophy,* Vol. 2, ed. Paul Edwards. New York: Macmillan, 1967.
G. MACDONALD ROSS, *Leibniz.* New York: Oxford University Press, 1984. Emphasizes the breadth of Leibniz's interests and contributions.
NICHOLAS RESCHER, *The Philosophy of Leibniz.* Englewood Cliffs, N.J.: Prentice-Hall, 1967. Systematic and comprehensive.
PAUL and ANNE MARTIN SCHRECKER, trans. and ed., *Monadology and Other Philosophical Essays.* Indianapolis: Bobbs-Merrill, 1965.
HARRY G. FRANKFURT, ed., *Leibniz: A Collection of Critical Essays.* Garden City, N.Y.: Doubleday, 1972.
VOLTAIRE (born François Marie Arouet), *Candide.* Many editions. The famous eighteenth-century satirical critique of Leibnizian optimism.

QUESTIONS

1. *Define:* rationalism, idealism, monad, apperception, contingent truths, necessary truths, existential proposition, principle of contradiction, principle of sufficient reason.

2. "It must be confessed that perception and its consequences are inexplicable by mechanical causes" (*Monadology,* Section 17). Paraphrase and discuss Leibniz's argument for this conclusion.

3. According to the *Monadology,* Section 23, "each perception can have no other natural origin but an antecedent perception, as every motion must be derived from one which preceded it." Would Spinoza agree? Would Descartes? Explain.

4. Judging from the text of the *Monadology,* was Leibniz what we called, in discussing Spinoza, a panpsychist?

5. How does Leibniz distinguish *memory* from *reason*?

6. What distinguishes human beings from mere animals, according to Leibniz?

7. How does a Leibnizian *monad* differ from a Cartesian *res cogitans*?

8. Analyze Leibniz's arguments to the existence and nature of God.

9.   How is God related to the world of monads? (In Spinoza's system, God is the *formal* and *material* cause of the world. What is God in Leibniz's system?)

10.   What is the difference between soul and body, according to Leibniz? And how does he explain their union?

11.   How did Leibniz manage to reconcile the Galilean (mechanistic) conception of nature with the Scholastic (teleological) conception?

NOTES

[1]He shares the credit with Sir Isaac Newton (1642–1727), who invented the calculus independently.

[2]Leibniz worked in the court of the Elector of Hanover.

[3]From "Letter to Queen Sophie Charlotte of Prussia," in Philip P. Wiener's *Leibniz Selections* (New York: Scribner's, 1951), pp. 355 and 359.

[4]From "Critical Remarks Concerning Descartes' Principles," in Paul and Anne Martin Schecker (ed. and trans.), *Monadology and Other Philosophical Essays*, pp. 41–42.

[5]Translated from the French by Frederick Henry Hedge. First appearing in the *Journal of Speculative Philosophy* of 1867, this translation was earlier reprinted in Benjamin Rand, ed., *Modern Classical Philosophers* (Cambridge, Mass.: Houghton Mifflin, 1924). I have added my own occasional minor changes and deletions to those of Rand.

[6]See p. 5, this volume.

[7]A term from Aristotle, meaning actualities.

[8]The "body" is *really* an organized complex of monads. "Entelechy" is here used to refer to the *dominant monad* in such a complex. (In other places, Leibniz uses "entelechy" as just another word for monad.)

chapter 4

LOCKE

ON THE ORIGIN AND LIMITS OF KNOWLEDGE

John Locke (1632–1704), born into an English Puritan family and educated in classics and medicine at Oxford University, became one of the most influential philosophers in history, especially through his *An Essay Concerning Human Understanding* and *Two Treatises of Government* (both published in 1690). Due to the liberalism, moderate optimism, and emphasis on experiment expressed in his writings, Locke was to become a hero of the great intellectual and cultural movement of the eighteenth century known as the Enlightenment.[1]

The *Essay* is a major attempt—the first in history—to define the limits of the human understanding by way of a detailed analysis of its powers.

> If by this enquiry into the nature of the understanding, I can discover the powers thereof, how far they reach, ... I suppose it may be of use to prevail with the busy mind of man to be more cautious in meddling with things exceeding its comprehension.... (I,i,4)[2]

The conclusion of the *Essay* is that there are indeed many more things exceeding the comprehension of the human mind than was allowed by the rationalist philosophies of Descartes, Spinoza, and Leibniz.

According to Locke, the foundation of all human understanding is the power to perceive *ideas* (understood as the direct objects of consciousness), and the power to perceive *relations* between ideas (similarity and difference, logical implication, etc.). In this Locke is in harmony with his rationalist predecessors. Where he differs from them is in his *empiricism*, that is in his view that all ideas, all the materials of knowledge, come from experience by way of the senses. He argued that even psychological ideas ("ideas of reflection"), such as the ideas of perceiving and thinking, depend on sense experience, since they are obtained only by the mind's reflection on its own reactions to, and operations upon, the ideas acquired through the five senses.

In addition to the passive powers of perception, human understanding is characterized, according to Locke, by three active powers: combination, comparison, and abstraction (see page 62). It is by means of these powers that other ideas are constructed out of the materials, or "simple ideas," of sensation and reflection.

The rationalists had maintained that there were certain ideas basic to the possibility of knowledge—in particular, the ideas of causality, substance, and God—which cannot possibly be derived from experience. Locke argues that we do *in fact* get the idea of causality from sense perception:

> In the notice that our senses take of the constant vicissitude of things, we cannot but observe that several particulars, both qualities and substances, begin to exist, and that they receive their existence from the due application and operation of some other being. From this operation we get our idea of cause and effect. (II, xxvi, 1)

As for *substance,* Locke admits that no clear and distinct idea of substance in general can be derived from experience, but he does not (like the rationalists) infer that it must derive from some other source (pure reason); he concludes that we simply do not have a clear and distinct conception of it.[3] As a corollary of that conclusion he developed a skepticism about whether psychological states and processes require a different sort of substance or underlying substratum from physical states and processes, a skepticism that shocked most of his contemporaries because it seemed to open the door to materialism, the view that all reality is ultimately physical. (See pp. 67–68 for a statement of Locke's argument.)

Even the idea of a Supreme Being is for Locke compounded out of simple ideas given in human experience:

> The degrees or extent wherein we ascribe existence, power, wisdom and all other perfections (which we can have any ideas of) to that sovereign Being, which we call God, being all boundless and infinite, we frame the best idea of him our minds are capable of: all which is done, I say, by enlarging those simple ideas we have taken from the operations of our own minds, by reflec-

tion; or by our senses, from exterior things, to that vastness to which infinity can extend them. (II, xxiii, 34)

Like Descartes, Locke was convinced that the existence of God can be proved. (His argument, quoted on p. 69, should be compared with those of Descartes.) Unlike Descartes, Locke did not base his confidence in the validity of the senses on an argument to the existence and goodness of God. Nor, as we have seen, did he allow that we have an innate idea of a Supreme Being.

Locke traces the fundamental limitation of human knowledge to its empirical origin. What man can know is relative to the ideas he can acquire through his senses over time—ideas which are often vague and indistinct and which seldom if ever give him insight into the real nature of things in the world. But this limitation, Locke assures us, is not to be much lamented:

> If we can find out those measures whereby a rational creature, put in the state in which man is in this world, may and ought to govern his opinions and actions depending thereupon, we need not be troubled that some other things escape our knowledge. (I,i,6)

What escapes our knowledge is a true *science* of natural substances, that is, rational insight into universal and necessary truths about the kinds of things existing in the natural world. For that would require perception of the *real essences* of things (i.e., of their internal constitutions), and this we lack because our senses are too weak to observe the minute particles which (according to Newton, and Locke following him) constitute all natural things. Thus, in natural philosophy (or natural science, as it is called today), we are "left only to OBSERVATION & EXPERIMENT" (IV,iii,28). This conclusion—one of the most characteristic and influential teachings of the *Essay*—is developed in passages such as the following:

> ... in the knowledge of bodies, we must be content to glean what we can from particular experiments: since we cannot, from a discovery of their real essences, grasp at a time whole sheaves, and in bundles comprehend the nature and properties of whole species together.... (IV, xii, 12)
>
> I doubt not but if we could discover the figure, size, texture, and motion of the minute constituent parts of any two bodies, we should know without trial several of their operations one upon another; as we do now the properties of a square or a triangle. Did we know the mechanical affections of the particles of rhubarb, hemlock, opium, and a man, as a watchmaker does those of a watch, whereby it performs its operations ..., we should be able to tell beforehand that rhubarb will purge, hemlock kill, and opium make a man sleep: as well as a watchmaker can, that a little piece of paper laid on the balance will keep the watch from going till it be removed.... But whilst we are destitute of senses acute enough to discover the minute particles of bodies, and to give us ideas of their mechanical affections, we must be content to be ignorant of their properties and ways of operation; nor can we be assured about them

any further than some few trials we make are able to reach. But whether they will succeed again another time, we cannot be certain. (IV,iii,25)

... He that, in the ordinary affairs of life, would admit of nothing but direct plain demonstration, would be sure of nothing in this world but of perishing quickly. The wholesomeness of his meat or drink would not give him reason to venture on it: and I would fain know what it is he could do upon such grounds as were capable of no doubt, no objection. (IV,xi,10)

Following a conception of science (*scientia*) that goes back to Descartes, and indeed to Aristotle, Locke says that there can be scientific knowledge only of those subjects about which there can be plain demonstrations from self-evident ("intuitively known") starting points. But Locke, departing at this point from the traditional view, denies that *nature* is a subject about which we can have such knowledge. His position is that, in the study of nature (as in most questions of religion and practical affairs), we must give up the search for science and aim for a more modest goal, namely the acquisition of relatively probable beliefs and the elimination of relatively improbable beliefs. Locke's picture of "the reasonable person" is of an individual with a just sense of his or her capacities and limits, knowing that the absolute certainties of *scientia* are rarely available to the human understanding, but that the formation of probable conjectures and reasonable convictions *are* normally within its reach. Such an individual views the Cartesian project as prideful and superfluous: prideful because it aspires to the Godlike view-point of absolute knowledge; superfluous because probabilities are a suffi-cient basis for improving our life on earth and for judging our moral duties. ("The candle that is set up in us shines bright enough for all our purposes" [I,i,5].)

Locke argues that it is only in mathematics and in ethics that we can attain to "plain demonstrations." In *these* subjects a knowledge of universal and necessary laws is within our grasp. But it is within our grasp only be-cause the objects of mathematical and ethical inquiry are *ideas* constructed by the mind after a plan of its own, rather than natural things, existing independently of the human mind. (See *Essay:* IV,iv,5–8.)

ON THE NATURE OF PERCEPTION

Following Aristotle, the Scholastics taught that there is nothing in the intel-lect that was not first in the senses. Descartes rejected this empiricist teach-ing; Locke reinstates it—but with a difference. Lockean epistemology dif-fers from Scholastic epistemology in that it combines empiricism with a theory of perception first defended by Descartes.

As you will recall from the Introduction, the Scholastics were naive realists, maintaining that physical objects are directly present to the mind in our sense experience of them. Locke parted company with them at this point, embarking on the New Way of Ideas. That is, he followed Descartes in maintaining that *ideas* are the only direct objects of sense experience. He also followed Descartes' representational–realist characterization of these ideas, according to which: (1) all are produced in the mind by the action of external (physical) causes on the senses; (2) all are images (representatives) of the physical causes which produced them; (3) some—the ideas of the primary qualities—are likenesses of the qualities inherent in physical objects; others—the ideas of the secondary qualities—are not (see pages 60–61).

According to Locke's diagnosis, the trouble with the Scholastics was not their reliance on sense experience but their *uncritical* reliance on it—an uncritical reliance which showed itself in their ascribing the "sensible species" of the secondary qualities of objects to the objects themselves. They thought, for example, that the heat one feels in the presence of a fire is a quality in the fire itself. They thereby confounded the nature of their own ideas with the nature of things themselves. As a cure for this uncritical empiricism, Dr. Locke prescribed a representative view of perception.

But how did Locke solve the problem inherent in representational realism, the so-called *problem of perception?*[4] He formulates this problem as follows:

> It is evident that the mind knows not things immediately, but only by the intervention of the *ideas* it has of them. *Our knowledge* therefore is *real* only so far as there is a conformity between our *ideas* and the reality of things. But what shall be here the criterion? How shall the mind, when it perceives nothing but its own *ideas,* know that they agree with things themselves? (IV,iv,3)

As an empiricist, Locke could not follow the Cartesian line of claiming to have certain nonempirical ideas (e.g., an innate idea of a nondeceiving Deity), which bridge the gap between ideas of sensation and things in the world. What line, or lines, Locke *did* take can be gathered from a close reading of relevant portions of his *Essay.*[5] The gist of his argument seems to be: (1) Physical causes must always be posited to explain our simple ideas, and so there will always be *some* conformity (at least) between our thoughts (which are analyzable into simple ideas) and things; (2) no one can doubt *in practice* that our senses inform us of a reality independent of our ideas. (A general impression: Locke doesn't seem to take the problem of perception with as much seriousness as Descartes had taken it. And this would seem to be in character for an empiricist, such as Locke. For an empiricist wants to accord to simple sense experiences a kind of validity so fundamental that it neither requires nor admits of proof.)

READING

FROM AN ESSAY CONCERNING HUMAN UNDERSTANDING

The Essay *is a very long work, comprising four Books: I, Of Innate Notions; II, Of Ideas; III, Of Words; IV, Of Knowledge and Opinion. The following selections are from Books II and IV.*

BOOK II–OF IDEAS

Chapter I. Of Ideas in General, and Their Original [Origin]

1. Every man being conscious to himself that he thinks; and that which his mind is applied about whilst thinking being the *ideas* that are there, it is past doubt that men have in their minds several ideas,—such as are those expressed by the words *whiteness, hardness, sweetness, thinking, motion, man, elephant, army, drunkenness,* and others: it is in the first place then to be inquired, *How he comes by them?* . . .

2. Let us then suppose the mind to be, as we say, white paper, void of all characters, without any ideas:—How comes it to be furnished? . . . . To this I answer, in one word, from EXPERIENCE. . . .

3. First, our senses, conversant about particular sensible objects, do convey into the mind several distinct perceptions of things, according to those various ways wherein those objects do affect them. And thus we come by those *ideas* we have of *yellow, white, heat, cold, soft, hard, bitter, sweet,* and all those which we call sensible qualities; which when I say the senses convey into the mind, I mean, they from external objects convey into the mind what produces there those perceptions. This great source of most of the ideas we have, depending wholly upon our senses, and derived [conveyed] by them to the understanding, I call SENSATION.

4. Secondly, the other fountain from which experience furnisheth the understanding with ideas is the perception of the operations of our own mind within us, as it is employed about the ideas it has got;—which operations, when the soul comes to reflect on and consider, do furnish the understanding with another set of ideas, which could not be had from things without. And such are *perception, thinking, doubting, believing, reasoning, knowing, willing,* and all the different actings of our own minds;—which we being conscious of, and observing in ourselves, do from these receive into our understandings as distinct ideas as we do from bodies affecting our senses. This source of ideas every man has wholly in himself; and though it be not sense, as having nothing to do with external objects, yet it is very like it, and might properly enough be called *internal sense.* But as I call the other sensation, so I call this REFLECTION, the ideas it affords being such only as the mind gets by reflecting on its own operations within itself. . . .

Chapter II. Of Simple Ideas

1.   ... Though the qualities that affect our senses are, in the things themselves, so united and blended, that there is no separation, no distance between them; yet it is plain, the ideas they produce in the mind enter by the senses simple and unmixed. For, though the sight and touch often take in from the same object, at the same, time, different ideas;—as a man sees at once motion and colour; the hand feels softness and warmth in the same piece of wax: yet the simple ideas thus united in the same subject, are as perfectly distinct as those that come in by different senses. The coldness and hardness which a man feels in a piece of ice being as distinct ideas in the mind as the smell and whiteness of a lily; or as the taste of sugar, and smell of a rose. And there is nothing [that] can be plainer to a man than the clear and distinct perception he has of those simple ideas; which, being each in itself uncompounded, contains in it nothing but *one uniform appearance, or conception in the mind,* and it is not distinguishable into different ideas.

2.   These simple ideas, the materials of all our knowledge, are suggested and furnished to the mind only by those two ways above mentioned, viz. sensation and reflection. When the understanding is once stored with these simple ideas, it has the power to repeat, compare, and unite them, even to an almost infinite variety, and so can make at pleasure new complex ideas. But it is not in the power of the most exalted wit, or enlarged understanding, by any quickness or variety of thought, to *invent* or *frame* one new simple idea in the mind, not taken in by the ways before mentioned: nor can any force of the understanding *destroy* those that are there. The dominion of man, in this little world of his own understanding being muchwhat the same as it is in the great world of visible things; wherein his power, however managed by art and skill reaches no farther than to compound and divide the materials that are made to his hand; but can do nothing towards the making the least particle of new matter, or destroying one atom of what is already in being. The same inability will every one find in himself, who shall be about to fashion in his understanding one simple idea, not received in by his senses from external objects, or by reflection from the operations of his own mind about them. I would have any one try to fancy any taste which had never affected his palate; or frame the idea of a scent he had never smelt: and when he can do this, I will also conclude that a blind man hath ideas of colours, and a deaf man true distinct notions of sounds.

Chapter VIII. Some Further Considerations Concerning our Simple Ideas of Sensation

8.   Whatsoever the mind perceives *in itself,* or is the immediate object of perception, thought, or understanding, that I call *idea*; and the power to produce any idea in our mind, I call *quality* of the subject wherein that power is. Thus a snowball having the power to produce in us the ideas of white, cold, and round,—the power to produce those ideas in us, as they are in the snowball, I call qualities; and as they are sensations or perceptions in our understandings, I call them ideas; which *ideas,* if I speak of sometimes as in the things themselves, I would be understood to mean those qualities in the objects which produce them in us.

9.   Qualities thus considered in bodies are,
     First, such as are utterly inseparable from the body, in what state soever

it be; and such as in all the alterations and changes it suffers, all the force can be used upon it, it constantly keeps; and such as sense constantly finds in every particle of matter which has bulk enough to be perceived; and the mind finds inseparable from every particle of matter, though less than to make itself singly be perceived by our senses: e.g. Take a grain of wheat, divide it into two parts; each part has still solidity, extension, figure, and mobility: divide it again, and it retains still the same qualities; and so divide it on, till the parts become insensible; they must retain still each of them all those qualities. For division (which is all that a mill, or pestle, or any other body does upon another, in reducing it to insensible parts) can never take away either solidity, extension, figure, or mobility from any body, but only makes two or more distinct separate masses of matter, of that which was but one before; all which distinct masses, reckoned as so many distinct bodies, after division, make a certain number. These I call *original* or *primary qualities* of body, which I think we may observe to produce simple ideas in us, viz. solidity, extention, figure, motion or rest, and number.

10. *Secondly,* such qualities which in truth are nothing in the objects themselves but powers to produce various sensations in us by their primary qualities, i.e. by the bulk, figure, texture, and motion of their insensible parts, as colours, sounds, tastes, &c. These I call *secondary qualities.* To these might be added a *third* sort, which are allowed to be barely powers; though they are as much real qualities in the subject as those which I, to comply with the common way of speaking, call qualities, but for distinction, secondary qualities. For the power in fire to produce a new colour, or consistency, in *wax* or *clay,*—by its primary qualities, is as much a quality in fire, as the power it has to produce in *me* a new idea or sensation of warmth or burning, which I felt not before,— by the same primary qualities, viz. the bulk, texture, and motion of its insensible parts.

Chapter IX. Of Perception

1. PERCEPTION, as it is the first faculty of the mind exercised about our ideas; so it is the first and simplest idea we have from reflection. . . .

2. What perception is, every one will know better by reflecting on what he does himself, when he sees, hears, feels, &c., or thinks, than by any discourse of mine. Whoever reflects on what passes in his own mind cannot miss it. And if he does not reflect, all the words in the world cannot make him have any notion of it.

3. This is certain, that whatever alterations are made in the body, if they reach not the mind; whatever impressions are made on the outward parts, if they are not taken notice of within, there is no perception. Fire may burn our bodies with no other effect than it does a billet, unless the motion be continued to the brain, and there the sense of heat, or idea of pain, be produced in the mind: wherein consists actual perception.

Chapter XII. Of Complex Ideas

1. We have hitherto considered those ideas, in the reception whereof the mind is only passive, which are those simple ones received from sensation and reflection. . . . But as the mind is wholly passive in the reception of all its simple ideas, so it exerts several acts of its own, whereby out of its simple ideas, as the materials and foundations of the rest, the others are framed. The

acts of the mind, wherein it exerts its power over its simple ideas, are chiefly these three: (1) Combining several simple ideas into one compound one; and thus all *complex ideas* are made. (2) The second is bringing two ideas, whether simple or complex, together, and setting them by one another, so as to take a view of them at once, without uniting them into one; by which way it gets all its *ideas of relations.* (3) The third is separating them from all other ideas that accompany them in their real existence: this is called abstraction: and thus all its *general ideas* are made. . . .

3. *Complex ideas,* however compounded and decompounded, though their number be infinite, and the variety endless, wherewith they fill and entertain the thoughts of men; yet I think they may be all reduced under these three heads:
    1. *Modes.*
    2. *Substances.*
    3. *Relations.*

4. First, *Modes* I call such complex ideas which, however compounded, contain not in them the supposition of subsisting by themselves, but are considered as dependences on, or affections of substances;—such as are the ideas signified by the words triangle, gratitude, murder, &c. . . .

6. Secondly, the ideas of *substances* are such combinations of simple ideas as are taken to represent distinct *particular* things subsisting by themselves; in which the supposed or confused idea of substance, such as it is, is always the first and chief. Thus if to substance be joined the simple idea of a certain dull whitish colour, with certain degrees of weight, hardness, ductility, and fusibility, we have the idea of lead; and a combination of the ideas of a certain sort of figure, with the powers of motion, thought and reasoning, joined to substance, make the ordinary idea of a man. Now of substances also, there are two sorts of ideas:—one of *single* substances, as they exist separately, as of a man or a sheep; the other of several of those put together, as an army of men, or flock of sheep—which *collective* ideas of several substances thus put together are as much each of them one single idea as that of a man or an unit.

7. Thirdly, the last sort of complex ideas is that we call *relation,* which consists in the consideration and comparing one idea with another.

Chapter XXI. Of Power

1. The mind being every day informed, by the senses, of the alteration of those simple ideas it observes in things without; and taking notice how one comes to an end, and ceases to be, and another begins to exist which was not before; reflecting also on what passes within itself, and observing a constant change of its ideas, sometimes by the impression of outward objects on the senses, and sometimes by the determination of its own choice; and concluding from what it has so constantly observed to have been, that the like changes will for the future be made in the same things, by like agents, and by the like ways,—considers in one thing the possibility of having any of its simple ideas changed, and in another the possibility of making that change; and so comes by that idea which we call *power.* Thus we say, fire has a power to melt gold, i.e. to destroy the consistency of its insensible parts, and consequently its hardness, and make it fluid; and gold has a power to be melted. . . . In which, and the like cases, the power we consider is in reference to the change of perceivable ideas. For we cannot observe any alteration to be made in, or operation upon anything, but by the observable change of its sensible ideas;

nor conceive any alteration to be made, but by conceiving a change of some of its ideas.

2. Power thus considered is two-fold, viz. as able to make, or able to receive any change. The one may be called *active,* and the other *passive* power. . . .

4. We are abundantly furnished with the idea of *passive* power by almost all sorts of sensible things. In most of them we cannot avoid observing their sensible qualities, nay, their very substances, to be in a continual flux. And therefore with reason we look on them as liable still to the same change. Nor have we of *active* power (which is the more proper signification of the word power) fewer instances. Since whatever change is observed, the mind must collect a power somewhere able to make that change, as well as a possibility in the thing itself to receive it. But yet, if we will consider it attentively, bodies, by our senses, do not afford us so clear and distinct an idea of active power, as we have from reflection on the operations of our minds. For all power relating to action, and there being but two sorts of action whereof we have an idea, viz. thinking and motion, let us consider whence we have the clearest ideas of the powers which produce these actions. (1) Of thinking, body affords us no idea at all; it is only from reflection that we have that. (2) Neither have we from body any idea of the beginning of motion. A body at rest affords us no idea of any active power to move; and when it is set in motion itself, that motion is rather a passion [something endured] than an action in it. For, when the ball obeys the motion of a billiard-stick, it is not any action of the ball, but bare passion. Also when by impulse it sets another ball in motion that lay in its way, it only communicates the motion it had received from another, and loses in itself so much as the other received: which gives us but a very obscure idea of an *active* power of moving in body, whilst we observe it only to *transfer,* but not *produce* any motion. For it is but a very obscure idea of power which reaches not the production of the action, but the continuation of the passion. For so is motion in a body impelled by another; the continuation of the alteration made in it from rest to motion being little more an action, than the continuation of the alternation of its figure by the same blow is an action. The idea of the *beginning* of motion we have only from reflection on what passes in ourselves; where we find by experience, that, barely by willing it, barely by a thought of the mind, we can move the parts of our bodies, which were before at rest. So that it seems to me, we have, from the observation of the operation of bodies by our senses, but a very imperfect obscure idea of *active* power; since they afford us not any idea in themselves of the power to begin any action, either motion or thought.

5. This, at least, I think evident,—That we find in ourselves a power to begin or forbear, continue or end several actions of our minds, and motions of our bodies, barely by a thought on preference of the mind ordering, or as it were commanding, the doing or not doing such or such a particular action. This power which the mind has thus to order the consideration of any idea, or the forbearing to consider it; or to prefer the motion of any part of the body to its rest, and *vice versa,* in any particular instance, is that which we call the *will.* The actual exercise of that power, by directing any particular action, or its forbearance, is that which we call *volition* or *willing.* . . . The power of perception is that which we call the *understanding.* Perception, which we make the act of the understanding, is of three sorts:—1. The perception of ideas in our minds. 2. The perception of the significance of signs. 3. The perception of the connexion or repugnancy, agreement or disagreement, that there is between any of our ideas. All these are attributed to the understanding, or per-

ceptive power, though it be the two latter only that use allows us to say we understand.

7. Everyone, I think, finds in himself a power to begin or forbear, continue or put an end to several actions in himself. From the consideration of the extent of this power of the mind over the actions of the man, which everyone finds in himself, arise the *ideas of liberty and necessity.*

Chapter XXIII. Of Our Complex Ideas of Substances

1. The mind being, as I have declared, furnished with a great number of the simple ideas, conveyed by the senses as they are found in exterior things, or by reflection on its own operations, takes notice also that a certain number of these simple ideas go constantly together; which being presumed to belong to one thing, and words being suited to common apprehensions, and made use of for quick dispatch, are called, so united in one subject, by one name; which, by inadvertency, we are apt afterward to talk of and consider as one simple idea, which indeed is a complication of many ideas together: because, as I have said, not imagining how these simple ideas *can* subsist by themselves, we accustom ourselves to suppose some *substratum* wherein they do subsist, and from which they do result, which therefore we call *substance.*

2. So that if any one will examine himself concerning his notion of pure sub-stance in general, he will find he has no other idea of it at all, but only a supposition of he knows not what *support* of such qualities which are capable of producing simple ideas in us; which qualities are commonly called acci-dents. If any one should be asked, what is the subject wherein color or weight inheres, he would have nothing to say, but the solid extended parts; and if he were demanded, what is it that solidity and extension inhere in, he would not be in a much better case than the Indian . . . who, saying that the world was supported by a great elephant, we asked what the elephant rested on; to which his answer was—a great tortoise: but being again pressed to know what gave support to the broad-backed tortoise, replied—*something, he knew not what.* And thus here, as in all other cases where we use words without having clear and distinct ideas, we talk like children: who, being questioned what such a thing is, which they know not, readily give this satisfactory answer, that it is *some-thing:* which in truth signifies no more, when so used, either by children or men, but that they know not what; and that the thing they pretend to know, and talk of, is what they have no distinct idea of at all, and so are perfectly ignorant of it, and in the dark. The idea then we have, to which we give the *general* name substance, being nothing but the supposed, but unknown, sup-port of those qualities we find existing, which we imagine cannot subsist *sine re substante,* [i.e.] without something to support them, we call that support *sub-stantia;* which, according to the true import of the word is, in plain English, standing under or upholding.

BOOK IV–OF KNOWLEDGE AND OPINION

Chapter I. Of Knowledge in General

1. Since the mind, in all its thoughts and reasonings, hath no other immediate object but its own ideas, which it alone does or can contemplate, it is evident that our knowledge is only conversant about them.

2. *Knowledge* then seems to me to be nothing but *the perception of the connexion of and agreement, or disagreement and repugnancy of any of our ideas.* In this alone it consists. Where this perception is, there is knowledge, and where it is not, there, though we may fancy, guess, or believe, yet we always come short of knowledge. . . .

3. But to understand a little more distinctly wherein this agreement or disagreement consists, I think we may reduce it all to these four sorts:

    I. *Identity,* or *diversity.*

    II. *Relation.*

    III. *Co-existence,* or *necessary connexion.*

    IV. *Real existence.*

4. As to the first sort of agreement or disagreement, viz. *identity* or *diversity.* It is the first act of the mind, when it has any sentiments or ideas at all, to perceive its ideas; and so far as it perceives them, to know each what it is, and thereby also to perceive their difference, and that one is not another. . . .

5. The next sort of agreement or disagreement the mind perceives in any of its ideas may, I think, be called *relative,* and is nothing but the perception of the *relation* between any two ideas, of what kind soever, whether substances, modes, or any other. For, since all distinct ideas must eternally be known not to be the same, and so be universally and constantly denied one of another, there could be no room for any positive knowledge at all, if we could not perceive any relation between our ideas, and find out the agreement or disagreement they have one with another, in several ways the mind takes of comparing them.

6. The third sort of agreement or disagreement to be found in our ideas, which the perception of the mind is employed about, is *co-existence* or *non-co-existence* in the *same subject;* and this belongs particularly to substances. Thus when we pronounce concerning gold, that it is fixed, our knowledge of this truth amounts to no more but this, that fixedness, or a power to remain in the fire unconsumed, is an idea that always accompanies and is joined with that particular sort of yellowness, weight, fusibility, malleableness, and solubility in *aqua regia,*[6] which make our complex idea signified by the word gold.

7. The fourth and last sort is that of *actual real existence* agreeing to any idea. Within these four sorts of agreement or disagreement is, I suppose, contained all the knowledge we have, or are capable of. For all the inquiries we can make concerning any of our ideas, all that we know or can affirm concerning any of them, is, That it is, or is not, the same with some other; that it does or does not always co-exist with some other idea in the same subject; that it has this or that relation with some other idea; or that it has a real existence without the mind. Thus, 'blue is not yellow,' is of identity. 'Two triangles upon equal bases between two parallels are equal,' is of relation. 'Iron is susceptible of magnetical impressions,' is of coexistence. 'God is,' is of real existence. . . .

Chapter II. Of the Degrees of Our Knowledge

1. . . . The different clearness of our knowledge seems to me to lie in the different way of perception the mind has of the agreement or disagreement of any of its ideas. For if we will reflect on our own ways of thinking, we will find, that sometimes the mind perceives the agreement or disagreement of two ideas *immediately by themselves,* without the intervention of any other: and this I think we may call *intuitive knowledge.* For in this the mind is at no pains of proving or examining, but perceives the truth as the eye doth light, only by

being directed towards it. Thus the mind perceives that *white* is not *black*, that a *circle* is not a *triangle*, that *three* are more than *two* and equal to *one and two.* Such kinds of truths the mind perceives at the first sight of the ideas together, by bare intuition; without the intervention of any other idea: and this kind of knowledge is the clearest and most certain that human frailty is capable of. . . . *It is on this intuition that depends all the certainty and evidence of all our knowledge.* . . .

2. The next degree of knowledge is, where the mind perceives the agreement or disagreement of any ideas, but not immediately. Though wherever the mind perceives the agreement or disagreement of any of its ideas, there be certain knowledge; yet it does not always happen, that the mind sees that agreement or disagreement, which there is between them, even where it is discoverable; and in that case remains in ignorance, and at most gets no further than a probable conjecture. The reason why the mind cannot always perceive presently the agreement or disagreement of two ideas, is, because those ideas, concerning whose agreement or disagreement the inquiry is made, cannot by the mind be so put together as to show it. In this case then, when the mind cannot so bring its ideas together as by their immediate comparison, and as it were juxta-position or application one to another, to perceive their agreement or disagreement, it is fain [required], *by the intervention of other ideas* . . . to discover the agreement or disagreement which it searches; and this is that which we call reasoning. Thus, the mind being willing to know the agreement or disagreement in bigness between the three angles of a triangle and two right ones, cannot by an immediate view and comparing them do it: because the three angles of a triangle cannot be brought at once, and be compared with any other one, or two, angles; and so of this the mind has no immediate, no intuitive knowledge. In this case the mind is fain to find out some other angles, to which the three angles of a triangle have an equality; and, finding those equal to two right ones, comes to know their equality to two right ones.

14. These two, viz. intuition and demonstration, are the degrees of our *knowledge;* whatever comes short of one of these, with what assurance soever embraced, is but *faith* or *opinion,* but not knowledge, at least in all general truths. There is, indeed, another perception of the mind, employed about *the particular existence of finite beings without us,* which, going beyond bare probability, and yet not reaching perfectly to either of the foregoing degrees of certainty, passes under the name of *knowledge.* There can be nothing more certain than that the idea we receive from an external object is in our minds: this is intuitive knowledge. But whether there be anything more than barely that idea in our minds; whether we can thence certainly infer the existence of anything without us, which corresponds to that idea, is that whereof some men think there may be a question made; because men may have such ideas in their minds, when no such thing exists, no such object affects their senses. But yet here I think we are provided with an evidence that puts us past doubting. For I ask any one, Whether he be not invincibly conscious to himself of a different perception, when he looks on the sun by day, and thinks on it by night; when he actually tastes wormwood, or smells a rose, or only thinks on that savour or odour? We as plainly find the difference there is between any idea revived in our minds by our own memory, and actually coming into our minds by our senses, as we do between any two distinct ideas. If any one say, a dream may do the same thing, and all these ideas may be produced in us without any external objects; he may please to dream that I make him this answer—1. That it is no great matter, whether I remove his scruple or no: where all is but

dream, reasoning and arguments are of no use, truth and knowledge nothing. 2. That I believe he will allow a very manifest difference between dreaming of being in the fire, and being actually in it. But yet if he be resolved to appear so sceptical as to maintain, that what I call being actually in the fire is nothing but a dream; and that we cannot thereby certainly know, that any such thing as fire actually exists without us: I answer, That we certainly finding, that pleasure or pain follows upon the application of certain objects to us, whose existence we perceive, or dream that we perceive, by our senses; this certainty is as great as our happiness or misery, beyond which we have no concernment to know or to be....

Chapter III. Of the Extent of Human Knowledge

1. Knowledge, as has been said, lying in the perception of the agreement or disagreement of any of our ideas, it follows from hence, That,
   First, we can have knowledge no further than we have *ideas*.
2. Secondly, That we can have no knowledge further than we can have *perception* of that agreement or disagreement. Which perception being: 1. Either by *intuition,* or the immediate comparing any two ideas; or, 2. By *reason,* examining the agreement or disagreement of two ideas, by the intervention of some others; or, 3. By *sensation,* perceiving the existence of particular things: hence it also follows:
3. Thirdly, That we cannot have an *intuitive knowledge* that shall extend itself to all our ideas, and all that we would know about them; because we cannot examine and perceive all the relations they have one to another, by juxtaposition, or an immediate comparison one with another. Thus, having the ideas of an obtuse and an acute angled triangle, both drawn from equal bases, and between parallels, I can, by intuitive knowledge, perceive the one not to be the other, but cannot that way know whether they be equal or no; because their agreement or disagreement in equality can never be perceived by an immediate comparing them; the difference of figure makes their parts incapable of an exact immediate application; and therefore there is need of some intervening qualities to measure them by, which is demonstration, or rational knowledge.
4. Fourthly, It follows, also, from what is above observed, that our *rational knowledge* cannot reach to the whole extent of our ideas: because between two different ideas we would examine, we cannot always find such mediums as we can connect one to another with an intuitive knowledge in all the parts of the deduction; and wherever that fails, we come short of knowledge and demonstration.
5. Fifthly, *Sensitive knowledge* reaching no further than the existence of things actually present to our senses, is yet much narrower than either of the former.
6. Sixthly, From all which it is evident, that the *extent of our knowledge* comes not only short of the reality of things, but even of the extent of our own ideas....
   We have ideas of a square, a circle, and equality, and yet, perhaps, shall never be able to find a circle equal to a square, and certainly know that it is so. We have the ideas of matter and thinking, but possibly shall never be able to know whether any mere material being thinks or no ... for I see no contradiction in it that the first eternal thinking Being should, if he pleased, give to certain

systems of created senseless matter, put together as he thinks fit, some degree of sense, perception, and thought . . .

Chapter IV. Of the Reality of our Knowledge

5. All our complex ideas, *except those of substances*, being archetypes [original patterns] of the mind's own making, not intended to be the copies of anything, nor referred to the existence of anything, as to their originals, cannot want [lack] any conformity necessary to real knowledge. For that which is not designed to represent anything but itself, can never be capable of a wrong representation, nor mislead us from the true apprehension of anything, by its dislikeness to it: and such, excepting those of substances, are all our complex ideas. Which, as I have showed in another place [II,v], are combinations of ideas, which the mind, by its free choice, puts together, without considering any connexion they have in nature. . . .

6. . . . The mathematician considers the truth and properties belonging to a rectangle or circle only as they are in idea in his own mind. For it is possible he never found either of them existing mathematically, i.e. precisely true, in his life. But yet the knowledge he has of any truths or properties belonging to a circle, or any other mathematical figure, are nevertheless true and certain, even of real things existing: because real things are no further concerned, nor intended to be meant by any such propositions, than as things really agree to those archetypes in his mind. Is it true of the *idea* of a triangle, that its three angles are equal to two right ones? It is true also of a triangle, wherever it *really exists*. . . .

7. And hence it follows that moral knowledge is as capable of real certainty as mathematics. For certainty being but the perception of the agreement or disagreement of our ideas, and demonstration nothing but the perception of such agreement, by the intervention of other ideas or mediums; our moral ideas, as well as mathematical, being archetypes themselves, and so adequate and complete ideas; all the agreement or disagreement which we shall find in them will produce real knowledge, as well as in mathematical figures.

8. For the attaining of knowledge and certainty, it is requisite that we have determined ideas: and, to make our knowledge real, it is requisite that the ideas answer their archetypes. Nor let it be wondered, that I place the certainty of our knowledge in the consideration of our ideas, with so little care and regard (as it may seem) to the real existence of things: since most of those discourses which take up the thoughts and engage the disputes of those who pretend to make it their business to inquire after truth and certainty, will, I presume, upon examination, be found to be general propositions, and notions in which existence is not at all concerned. All the discourses of the mathematicians about the squaring of a circle, conic sections, or any other part of mathematics, concern not the existence of any of those figures: but their demonstrations, which depend on their ideas, are the same, whether there be any square or circle existing in the world or no. In the same manner, the truth and certainty of moral discourses abstracts from the lives of men, and the existence of those virtues in the world whereof they treat. . . . If it be true in speculation, i.e. in idea, that murder deserves death, it will also be true in reality of any action that exists conformable to that idea of murder. As for other actions, the truth of that proposition concerns them not. And thus it is of all other

species of things, which have no other essences but those ideas which are in the minds of men.

Chapter X. Of Our Knowledge of the Existence of a God

2. I think it is beyond question, that man has a clear idea of his own being; he knows certainly he exists, and that he is something. . . .

3. In the next place, man knows, by an intuitive certainty, that bare *nothing can no more produce any real being, than it can be equal to two right angles.* If a man knows not that nonentity, or the absence of all being, cannot be equal to two right angles, it is impossible he should know any demonstration in Euclid. If, therefore, we know there is some real being, and that nonentity cannot produce any real being, it is an evident demonstration, that *from eternity there has been something;* since what was not from eternity had a beginning; and what had a beginning must be produced by something else.

4. Next, it is evident, that what had its being and beginning from another, must also have all that which is in and belongs to its being from another too. All the powers it has must be owing to and received from the same source. This eternal source, then, of all being must also be the source and original of all power; and so *this eternal Being must be also the most powerful.*

5. Again, a man finds in *himself* perception and knowledge. We have then got one step further; and we are certain now that there is not only some being, but some knowing, intelligent being in the world. There was a time, then, when there was no knowing being, and when knowledge began to be; or else there has been also *a knowing being from eternity.* If it be said, there was a time when no being had any knowledge, when that eternal being was void of all understanding; I reply, that then it was impossible there should ever have been any knowledge: it being as impossible that things wholly void of knowledge, and operating blindly, and without any perception, should produce a knowing being, as it is impossible that a triangle should make itself three angles bigger than two right ones. For it is as repugnant to the idea of senseless matter, that it should put into itself sense, perception, and knowledge, as it is repugnant to the idea of a triangle, that it should put into itself greater angles than two right ones.

6. Thus, from the consideration of ourselves, and what we infallibly find in our own constitutions, our reason leads us to the knowledge of this certain and evident truth,—*That there is an eternal, most powerful, and most knowing Being.* . . .

Chapter XI. Of Our Knowledge of the Existence of Other Things

1. The knowledge of our own being we have by intuition. The existence of a God, reason clearly makes known to us, as has been shown.

   The knowledge of the existence of *any other thing* we can have only by *sensation:* for there being no necessary connexion of real existence with any *idea* a man hath in his memory; nor of any other existence but that of God with the existence of any particular man: no particular man can know the existence of any other being, but only when, by actual operating upon him, it makes itself perceived by him. For, the having the idea of anything in our mind, no more proves the existence of that thing, than the picture of a man evidences his being in the world, or the visions of a dream make thereby a true history.

2. It is therefore the *actual receiving* of ideas from without that gives us notice of the existence of other things, and makes us know, that something doth exist at that time without us, which causes that idea in us; though perhaps we neither know nor consider how it does it. For it takes not from the certainty of our senses, and the ideas we receive by them, that we know not the manner wherein they are produced: e.g. whilst I write this, I have, by the paper affecting my eyes, that idea produced in my mind, which, whatever object causes, I call *white;* by which I know that that quality or accident (i.e. whose appearance before my eyes always causes that idea) doth really exist, and hath a being without me. And of this, the greatest assurance I can possibly have, and to which my faculties can attain, is the testimony of my eyes, which are the proper and sole judges of this thing; whose testimony I have reason to rely on as so certain, that I can no more doubt, whilst I write this, that I see white and black, and that something really exists that causes that sensation in me, than that I write or move my hand; which is a certainty as great as human nature is capable of, concerning the existence of anything, but a man's self alone, and of God.

3. ... But besides the assurance we have from our senses themselves, that they do not err in the information they give us of the existence of things without us, when they are affected by them, we are further confirmed in this assurance by other concurrent reasons:

4. I. It is plain those perceptions are produced in us by exterior causes affecting our senses: because those that want the *organs* of any sense, never can have the ideas belonging to that sense produced in their minds. This is too evident to be doubted: and therefore we cannot but be assured that they come in by the organs of that sense, and no other way. The organs themselves, it is plain, do not produce them: for then the eyes of a man in the dark would produce colours. ...

5. II. Because sometimes I find that *I cannot avoid having those ideas produced in my mind.* ... [I]f I turn my eyes at noon towards the sun, I cannot avoid the ideas which the light or sun then produces in me. So that there is a manifest difference between the ideas laid up in my memory, (over which, if they were there only, I should have constantly the same power to dispose of them, and lay them by at pleasure) and those which force themselves upon me, and I cannot avoid having. And therefore it must needs be some exterior cause, and the brisk acting of some objects without me, whose efficacy I cannot resist, that produces those ideas in my mind, whether I will or no. Besides, there is nobody who doth not perceive the difference in himself between contemplating the sun, as he hath the idea of it in his memory, and actually looking upon it: of which two, his perception is so distinct, that few of his ideas are more distinguishable one from another. And therefore he hath certain knowledge that they are not *both* memory, or the actions of his mind, and fancies only within him; but that actual seeing hath a cause without.

8. But yet, if after all this any one will be so sceptical as to distrust his senses, and to affirm that all we see and hear, feel and taste, think and do, during our whole being, is but the series and deluding appearances of a long dream, whereof there is no reality; and therefore will question the existence of all

things, or our knowledge of anything: I must desire him to consider, that, if all be a dream, then he doth but dream that he makes the question, and so it is not much matter that a waking man should answer him. But yet, if he pleases, he may dream that I make him this answer, That the certainty of things existing in *rerum natura* [the nature of things] when we have the testimony of our senses for it is not only as great as our frame [nature] can attain to, but as our condition needs. For, our faculties being suited not to the full extent of being, nor to a perfect, clear, comprehensive knowledge of things free from all doubt and scruple; but to the preservation of us, in whom they are; and accommodated to the use of life: they serve to our purpose well enough, if they will but give us certain notice of those things, which are convenient or inconvenient to us. For he that sees a candle burning, and hath experimented [experienced] the force of its flame by putting his finger to it, will little doubt that this is something existing without him, which does him harm, and puts him to great pain: which is assurance enough, when no man requires greater certainty to govern his actions by than what is as certain as his actions themselves. And if our dreamer pleases to try whether the glowing heat of a glass furnace be barely a wandering imagination in a drowsy man's fancy, by putting his hand into it, he may perhaps be wakened into a certainty greater than he could wish, that it is something more than bare imagination. So that this evidence is as great as we can desire, being as certain to us as our pleasure or pain, i.e. happiness or misery; beyond which we have no concernment, either of knowing or being. Such an assurance of the existence of things without us is sufficient to direct us in attaining the good and avoiding the evil which is caused by them, which is the important concernment we have of being made acquainted with them.

Chapter XVIII. Of Faith and Reason, and Their Distinct Provinces

1. It has been above shown, 1. That we are of necessity ignorant, and want [lack] knowledge of all sorts, where we want ideas. 2. That we are ignorant, and want rational knowledge, where we want proofs. 3. That we want certain knowledge and certainty, as far as we want clear and determined specific ideas. 4. That we want probability to direct our assent in matters where we have neither knowledge of our own nor testimony of other men to bottom [base] our reason upon.

    From these things thus premised, I think we may come to lay down *the measures and boundaries between faith and reason:* the want whereof may possibly have been the cause, if not of great disorders, yet at least of great disputes, and perhaps mistakes in the world. For till it be resolved how far we are to be guided by reason, and how far by faith, we shall in vain dispute, and endeavour to convince one another in matters of religion.

2. I find every sect, as far as reason will help them, make use of it gladly: and where it fails them, they cry out, It is matter of faith, and above reason. And I do not see how they can argue with any one, or ever convince a gainsayer who makes use of the same plea, without setting down strict boundaries between faith and reason; which ought to be the first point established in all questions where faith has anything to do.

    Reason, therefore, here, as contradistinguished to *faith,* I take to be the discovery of the certainty or probability of such propositions or truths, which the mind arrives at by deduction made from such ideas, which it has got by the use of its natural faculties; viz. by sensation or reflection.

Faith, on the other side, is the assent to any proposition, not thus made out by the deductions of reason, but upon the credit of the proposer, as coming from God, in some extraordinary way of communication. This way of discovering [revealing] truths to men, we call *revelation.*

10.   ... Whatever God hath revealed is certainly true: no doubt can be made of it. This is the proper object of faith: but whether it be a *divine* revelation or no, reason must judge; which can never permit the mind to reject a greater evidence to embrace what is less evident, nor allow it to entertain probability in opposition to knowledge and certainty. There can be no evidence that any traditional revelation is of divine origin, in the words we receive it, and in the sense we understand it, so clear and so certain as that of the principles of reason: and therefore *Nothing that is contrary to, and inconsistent with, the clear and self-evident dictates of reason, has a right to be urged or assented to as a matter of faith, wherein reason hath nothing to do....*

11.   If the provinces of faith and reason are not kept distinct by these boundaries, there will, in matter of religion, be no room for reason at all; and those extravagant opinions and ceremonies that are to be found in the several religions of the world will not deserve to be blamed. For, to this crying up of faith in *opposition* to reason, we may, I think, in good measure ascribe those absurdities that fill almost all the religions which possess and divide mankind. For men having been principled with an opinion, that they must not consult reason in the things of religion, however apparently contradictory to common sense and the very principles of all their knowledge, have let loose their fancies and natural superstition; and have been by them led into so strange opinions, and extravagant practices in religion, that a considerate man cannot but stand amazed at their follies, and judge them so far from being acceptable to the great and wise God, that he cannot avoid thinking them ridiculous and offensive to a sober good man. So that, in effect, religion, which should most distinguish us from beasts, and ought most peculiarly to elevate us, as rational creatures, above brutes, is that wherein men often appear irrational, and more senseless than beasts themselves....

FOR FURTHER READING

GILBERT RYLE, "John Locke on the Human Understanding," in *Locke and Berkeley,* C. B. Martin and D. M. Armstrong, eds. Garden City, N.Y.: Doubleday, 1968. Brings out the distinctive features of Locke's epistemology.

JOHN J. JENKINS, *Understanding Locke: An Introduction to Philosophy Through John Locke's Essay.* Edinburgh: Edinburgh University Press, 1983. Highly recommended.

R. S. WOOLHOUSE, *Locke.* Minneapolis: University of Minnesota Press, 1983. Woolhouse interprets the major themes in the *Essay* and discusses them against the intellectual background of the age.

JOHN DUNN, *Locke.* New York: Oxford University Press, 1984. Emphasizes the political theory in, and the social setting of, Locke's work.

G. W. LEIBNIZ, *New Essays On Human Understanding,* trans. and ed. by P. Remnant and Jonathan Bennett. Cambridge: Cambridge University Press, 1982 (abridged ed.). The classic rationalist critique of Locke.

P. H. NIDDITCH, ed., *John Locke: An Essay Concerning Human Understanding.* Oxford: Oxford University Press, 1975. The definitive edition of the *Essay.* Contains a useful introduction.

QUESTIONS

1. *Define:* idea, idea of sensation, idea of reflection, simple idea, complex idea, primary quality, secondary quality, mode, substance, knowledge.

2. State and explain: (a) the four kinds of agreement or disagreement between ideas, (b) the three degrees of our knowledge.

3. Summarize and evaluate Locke's argument for the existence of an "eternal, most powerful, and most knowing Being."

4. "That sense perceptions are produced in us by exterior causes affecting our senses is plain from the fact that those who lack the *organs* of any sense, such as eyes for seeing, never have the ideas belonging to that sense produced in their minds" (*Essay* IV,xi,4: paraphrased). Explain the *circularity* in the preceding argument. Can you find a better argument in Locke for the proposition that sense experience proves the existence of "things without us"?

5. Summarize and discuss Locke's account of the proper relationship between reason and religious faith.

6. Review the section of Chapter 1 entitled "Some Major Issues of Modern Philosophy" and then try to explain Locke's position on each issue and how (if at all) it differs from the positions of the earlier philosophers in our study.

7. Evaluate Locke's account of the origin of the ideas of *cause and effect* and of *active and passive power.*

8. Locke insists on the impossibility of inventing or imagining a new *simple* idea. But how is it that he can be so sure that no one could possibly, for example, "fancy any taste which had never affected his palate, or frame the idea of a scent he had never smelt" (II,ii,2)? Suppose someone insisted that *she* could imagine such a scent or taste. Could Locke refute her?

9. A dog perceives, yet has no idea of what perception *is.* Is this because he cannot reflect (as we can) on his acts of perception? Suppose *we* are told to reflect on our acts of perception: We wouldn't be able to obey this order unless we already knew what is meant by "perception"; for, if we didn't know that, we wouldn't know *what* it is we were supposed to be reflecting on.

How does the preceding line of thinking bear on what Locke says in II,ix,2 about the origin of the "simple idea of perception"?

10. "Whatever alterations are made in the body, if they do not reach the mind . . . there is no perception" (II,ix,3). What kind of statement is Locke making here? Is it like: "Whatever fuel is put into the tank, if it doesn't reach the combustion chambers, there is no starting the engine"? Or is it more like: "Whatever figure is drawn on the board, if it doesn't have four sides, there is no rectangle"?

11. Drawing on material from Dunn (see For Further Reading), prepare a report on Locke's political thought.

12. Discuss the following claims: (a) Locke's campaign against the epistemological doctrine of innate ideas is paralleled by his campaign against the political doctrine of the divine right of kings; (b) "The idea that, ultimately, I depend on nothing but my own sensations for my vision of the world no doubt appeals to the entrepreneural spirit. Empiricism is perhaps the appropriate

epistemology for a private enterprise economy" (Fergus Kerr, *Theology After Wittgenstein* [Oxford: Blackwell, 1986], p. 132).

NOTES

[1]The Enlightenment was concerned with the rational examination of traditional doctrines and institutions. Among its outstanding shapers and agents were the Frenchmen Voltaire and Diderot, the Scots Hume and Adam Smith, the Americans Franklin and Jefferson, and the Germans Lessing and Kant. "Have the courage to use your own understanding!" That, as Kant put it, was the motto of the Enlightenment.

Representing the modern spirit of critical individualism, as opposed to the credulous traditionalism associated with the Dark Ages, Locke and the other seventeenth-century philosophers were important precursors of the Enlightenment.

[2]"I,i,4" means "Book I, Chapter I, Section 4 of the *Essay*."

[3]See p. 64 Cf. Elliot D. Cohen, "Reason and Experience in Locke's Epistemology," *Philosophy and Phenomenological Research*, XLV (1984), p. 75.

[4]See p. 6.

[5]Reprinted on pp. 66–67 (#14) and 69–70.

[6]*Aqua regia* means royal water. It refers to a mixture of nitric and hydrochloric acids which dissolves gold, the royal metal.

chapter 5

BERKELEY

IDEALIST EMPIRICISM

George Berkeley (1685–1753) was born and educated in Ireland. After studies at Trinity College, Dublin, he took holy orders in the Anglican Church. He spent a few years in the New World in an unsuccessful attempt to found a missionary college. A few years after his return to Europe, he was made Bishop of the Irish diocese of Cloyne. At the time of his death, in Oxford, England, he was more highly esteemed for his work as a bishop than for his philosophical works, which were deemed eccentric and paradoxical by many thinkers of the time.

Berkeley agreed with Locke's empiricist epistemology but disagreed with his realist metaphysics. In the *Treatise Concerning the Principles of Human Knowledge* (1710) and the *Three Dialogues Between Hylas and Philonous* (1713), Berkeley argued that *idealism* is the only metaphysics consistent with empiricism. Idealism ("immaterialism," as Berkeley called it) says that only minds and their ideas are real. Empiricism (as you will recall from the last chapter) says that all ideas come from experience by way of the senses. Now, according to Berkeley, Locke's claim that our complex idea of a thing includes the idea of an unperceiveable material substratum in which its perceptible

qualities inhere is without foundation in experience and therefore inconsistent with his professed empiricism.

Berkeley is at pains to assure us that immaterialism is consistent with
common sense—that it is not eccentric and paradoxical, as his critics
charged. Witness the following from the *Principles:*

> That the things I see with my eyes and touch with my hands do exist, really
> exist, I make not the least question. The only thing whose existence we deny
> is that which *philosophers* [such as Locke] call matter or corporeal substance.
> And in [the] doing of this, there is no danger done to the rest of mankind,
> who, I dare say, will never miss it. (Sec. 35)

Berkeley did not want to deny *that* shoes, ships, and sealing wax and other
objects exist. He simply wanted to clarify *what* the existence of such things
amounts to. And his major conclusion was that their existence consists in
their being *objects of perception,* i.e., ideas. These objects he contrasted with
the *perceiving subjects* (minds, spirits) on whose activities (perceiving, willing)
they depend.

Locke said that corporeal objects are the *causes* of our ideas. Berkeley
rejected this realist view as incompatible with the common-sense truism that
we *see* or *immediately perceive* objects, without having to infer their existence
from something else. For we do not, according to Berkeley, immediately
perceive the *causes* of our ideas. Yet our ideas *do* have causes, Berkeley admitted. And, as these causes cannot be "imperceptible *corporeal* things" (a contradiction in terms for Berkeley), they must be some "imperceptible, *incorporeal* things" ("spirits"). "Take here in brief my meaning," says Berkeley
("Philonous") in the Second of the *Three Dialogues Between Hylas and Philonous:*

> It is evident that the things I perceive are my own ideas, and that no idea can
> exist unless it be in a mind. Nor is it less plain that these ideas or things by
> me perceived, either themselves or their archetypes [patterns], exist indepen-
> dently of my mind; since I know myself not to be their author, it being not in
> my power to determine at pleasure what particular ideas I shall be affected
> with upon opening my eyes or ears. They must therefore exist in some other
> mind, whose will it is they should be exhibited to me. The things, I say, imme-
> diately perceived are ideas or sensations, call them which you will. But how
> can any idea or sensation exist in, or be produced by, anything but a mind or
> spirit? This indeed is inconceivable. . . . [1]

Berkeley equates causality with will power. So the only true causes are spirits, things with volition, i.e. wills of their own. Other things, namely ideas,
are causally inert. There is, indeed, a certain regularity in the sequence of
ideas. For example, the idea of smoke *regularly follows upon* the idea of fire.
But this is not to say that the latter idea *causes* the former.[2]

The order and regularity observable in that wondrous series of ideas that we call "the course of nature" can be accounted for only by reference to the will of a supremely wise and powerful spirit, namely God. God is the author of the laws of nature, that is, of the rules governing the succession of our sense perceptions. But, since we have no insight into the divine will, we must learn the laws of nature by way of sense experience, "which teaches us that such and such ideas are attended with such and such other ideas in the ordinary course of things" (*Principles*, Sec. 30).

PHILOSOPHY OF SCIENCE

Berkeley sees no incompatibility between the work of natural philosophers (experimental scientists) and a sound metaphysical philosophy (his own immaterialism): Natural philosophers are simply discovering regularities in the succession of our ideas. Nor does he see any conflict between natural philosophy, properly understood, and everyday, common-sense judgments: natural philosophers are simply doing, in a more systemtic way, what we all do when, in the course of experience, we form empirical generalizations and make predictions on the basis of them.

> If therefore we consider the difference there is betwixt natural philosophers and other men with regard to their knowledge of the phenomena, we shall find it consists not in an exacter knowledge of the *efficient cause* that produces them—for *that* can be no other than the *will of a spirit*—but only in a greater largeness of comprehension, whereby analogies, harmonies, and agreements are discovered in the works of nature, and the particular effects explained, that is, *reduced to general rules;* which rules, grounded on the analogy and uniformness observed in the production of natural effects, ... extend our prospect beyond what is present and near to us, and enable us to make very probable conjectures touching things that may have happened at very great distances of time and place, as well as to predict things to come.... (*Principles,* Sec. 105)

The metaphysician seeks to tell us about the ultimate principles and causes of things, including their real efficient cause, i.e., the agent or agents that produced them and holds them in being. The natural philosopher, on the other hand, has the job of providing us with a kind of synoptic description of observed phenomena, a description useful for the prediction and control of experience. *Explanations* in natural philosophy are, typically, nothing but a matter of relating particular phenomena to general rules, or *laws of nature.* Thus we can account for the fact that a certain bottle of liquid fizzes when shaken by referring to the fact that it is carbonated, and to the rule that all carbonated liquids fizz when shaken. And thus Newton accounted for the fall of apples, the ebb and flow of tides, etc. by representing them as special cases of a single regularity, namely the law of gravity:

$$F = G \frac{mm'}{D^2}$$

Berkeley applauded the achievements of Sir Isaac Newton and of other modern students of nature. But he thought that some of Newton's followers had misunderstood the theory of gravitation, interpreting the gravitational constant (G) as the name of some mysterious force that causes apples to fall, etc. To say that the acceleration of a falling apple is caused by the force of gravity is to say nothing more illuminating than Moliére's doctor said when asked why opium puts us to sleep: "It puts us to sleep because of its dormitive power."

Berkeley wanted to demystify the accomplishments of the physicists. The term "gravitational attraction" is a convenient way of referring to a common feature of a large range of phenomena; it is not a (dubious) hypothesis about their efficient cause. Similarly, words like "corpuscle" and "atom" are useful devices in our efforts to briefly sum up certain experimental findings, but there is no need to construe them as names for mysterious, imperceivable material causes. The theoretical terms in science, such as atom, should not be read as standing for existing things, any more than meridian lines on a globe should be read as naming actual lines on the surface of the earth, or than "the average woman" should be construed as standing for an individual over and above Mary, Nan, Olga, etc.

Berkeley's original and influential philosophy of science is known as *instrumentalism*. This is the view that those terms in a scientific theory that appear to postulate unobservable entities are really just instruments or tools that have been found useful for the summation of experience. Just as the notion of meridian lines helps us to organize geographical data, so the notion of atoms (with the accompanying pictures of minute billiard ball–like particles) helps us to organize experimental data about the behavior of gasses, etc.

Although an admirer of Newton, Berkeley found a few of his teachings unacceptable—notably, the doctrine of absolute space. In the *Mathematical Principles of Natural Philosophy* (1687) Newton had said: "Absolute space in its own nature, without relation to anything external, remains always similar and immovable. . . . " Berkeley argues, in Sections 110–117 of the *Principles,* that Newton is here talking nonsense—that his talk of absolute space, and of motion in this absolute space, has neither empirical content nor instrumental value. The following passages convey the gist of his critique:

> . . . [I]t does not appear to me that there can be any motion other than *relative;* so that to conceive motion there must be conceived at least two bodies,

whereof the distance or position in regard to each other is varied. Hence, if there was only one body in being it could not possibly be moved. This to me seems very evident, in that the idea I have of motion does necessarily include relation. (Sec. 112)

... [T]he philosophic consideration of motion does not imply the being of an *absolute space,* distinct from that which is perceived by sense and related to bodies.... And perhaps, if we inquire narrowly, we shall find we cannot even frame an idea of *pure space* exclusive of all body.... When I excite a motion in some part of my body, if it be free or without resistance, I say there is *space;* but if I find a resistance, then I say there is *body;* and in proportion as the resistance to motion is lesser or greater, I say the space is more or less *pure.* So that when I speak of pure or empty space, it is not to be supposed that the word "space" stands for an idea distinct from or conceivable without body and motion—though indeed we are apt to think every noun substantive stands for a distinct idea that may be separated from all others; which has occasioned infinite mistakes. When, therefore, supposing all the world to be annihilated besides my own body, I say there still remains *pure space,* thereby nothing else is meant but only that I conceive it possible for the limbs of my body to be moved on all sides without the least resistance; but if that too were annihilated then there could be no motion, and consequently no space. (Sec. 116)

This critique was a stimulus to Ernst Mach (1838–1916) and Albert Einstein (1879–1955) in their development of relativity physics.[3]

ARGUMENTS FOR IDEALISM

Models of concise and lucid prose, Berkeley's writings often can be distilled into series of short, step-by-step arguments. Let me illustrate this by setting out some of the more important arguments contained in the excerpt from the *Principles* which is the reading for this chapter.

Section 4: Houses, trees, etc. are sensible objects. Sensible objects are perceived by sense.

Everything perceived by sense is an idea or combination of ideas.

No ideas or combination of ideas exist unperceived.

Thus, no houses, trees, etc. exist unperceived.

Section 8: No ideas exist without the mind, i.e., unperceived.

Everything that resembles an idea is another idea.

Therefore, nothing that resembles an idea exists without the mind.

The preceding argument, known as *Berkeley's Syllogism,* is supposed to refute representational realism, according to which some of our ideas resemble the qualities of external, material things. Berkeley defends the second premise of his syllogism with the following subargument:

> If the qualities of which our ideas are supposed to be representations are perceivable, then they are really ideas.
>
> If those qualities are not perceivable, then they can be nothing like ideas.
>
> They are either perceivable or imperceptible.
>
> Therefore, either they are ideas, or they are nothing like ideas.

In Sections 9–15, Berkeley explicitly attacks the distinction that representational realists want to make between primary and secondary qualities of bodies. I will leave it to the reader to analyze these arguments, and also the argument of Sections 16–17, which seeks to demonstrate the meaninglessness of Locke's notion of material substance. (Review p. 64, "Of our Complex Ideas of Substances," as well as Locke's way of making the primary/secondary quality distinction, pp. 60–61.)

Section 18:   If we know that material things exist outside the mind corresponding to the ideas which we have of them, then we know this *either* immediately (by sense) *or* mediately (by reasoning).

We don't know this by sense (for only ideas are known immediately).

We don't know it by reasoning (what happens in dreams shows it "possible we might be affected with all the ideas we have now though there were no bodies existing without, resembling them").

Therefore, we cannot know that material things exist outside the mind corresponding to our ideas.

This is known as an *epistemological argument* for immaterialism. For its conclusion is not (as with the preceding, *metaphysical arguments*) that material substances do not (or cannot) *exist,* but rather the weaker conclusion that we could never *know* they exist.

Section 19:   A good explanatory hypothesis must be comprehensible.

The material substance hypothesis, which involves the notion that something material (bodies) acts upon the immaterial (mind), is incomprehensible.

Therefore, that hypothesis is not a good explanation.

Here Berkeley is addressing the suggestion that the *material substance hypothesis* provides the best (if not the only possible) explanation of the presence of ideas of sensation in our minds. He responds by invoking the mind/body problem, reminding us that even believers in matter "own themselves unable to comprehend in what manner body can act upon spirit."

Sections 22–24: No objects of thought can be conceived as existing without the mind.

Bodies are objects of thought.

Thus, bodies cannot be conceived as existing without the mind.

This is known as the *inconceivability argument*. Whether it (or any of the preceding arguments) is *sound* is a good question for discussion. (A sound argument is one whose conclusion follows from true premises.)

In the excerpted text, subsequent to the inconceivability argument, Berkeley talks about causality, spirit, laws of nature, God, and the notion of a real thing. These topics (all but the last) were touched on earlier. The reader is urged to analyze what Berkeley has to say about them.

READING

FROM A TREATISE CONCERNING THE PRINCIPLES OF HUMAN KNOWLEDGE

1. It is evident to any one who takes a survey of the *objects of human knowledge,* that they are either *ideas* actually imprinted on the senses; or else such as are perceived by attending to the passions and operations of the mind; or lastly, *ideas* formed by help of memory and imagination—either compounding, dividing, or barely representing those originally perceived in the aforesaid ways. By sight I have the ideas of light and colours, with their several degrees and variations. By touch I perceive hard and soft, heat and cold, motion and resistance, and of all these more and less either as to quantity or degree. Smelling furnishes me with odours; the palate with tastes; and hearing conveys sounds to the mind in all their variety of tone and composition. And as several of these are observed to accompany each other, they come to be marked by one name, and so to be reputed as one thing. Thus, for example, a certain colour, taste, smell, figure, and consistence having been observed to go together, are accounted one distinct thing, signified by the name *apple;* other collections of ideas constitute a stone, a tree, a book, and the like sensi-

ble things; which as they are pleasing or disagreeable excite the passions of love, hatred, joy, grief, and so forth.

2. But, besides all that endless variety of ideas or objects of knowledge, there is likewise something which knows or perceives them, and exercises divers operations, [such] as willing, imagining, remembering, about them. This perceiving, active being is what I call *mind, spirit, soul,* or *myself.* By which words I do not denote any one of my ideas, but a thing entirely distinct from them, wherein they exist, or, which is the same thing, whereby they are perceived—for the existence of an idea consists in being perceived.

3. That neither our thoughts, nor passions, nor ideas formed by the imagination, exist without the mind, is what everybody will allow. And to me it is no less evident that the various sensations, or ideas imprinted on the sense, however blended or combined together (that is, whatever objects they compose), cannot exist otherwise than in a mind perceiving them.—I think an intuitive knowledge may be obtained of this by any one that shall attend to what is meant by the term *exist,* when applied to sensible things. The table I write on I say exists, that is, I see and feel it; and if I were out of my study I should say it existed—meaning thereby that if I was in my study I might perceive it, or that some other spirit actually does perceive it. There was an odour, that is, it was smelt; there was a sound, that is, it was heard; a colour or figure, and it was perceived by sight or touch. This is all that I can understand by these and the like expressions. For as to what is said of the absolute existence of unthinking things without any relation to their being perceived, that is to me perfectly unintelligible. Their *esse* is *percipi* ["to be" is "to be perceived"], nor is it possible they should have any existence out of the minds of thinking things which perceive them.

4. It is indeed an opinion strangely prevailing amongst men, that houses, mountains, rivers, and in a word all sensible objects, have an existence, natural or real, distinct from their being perceived by the understanding. But, with how great an assurance and acquiescence soever this principle may be entertained in the world, yet whoever shall find in his heart to call it in question may, if I mistake not, perceive it to involve a manifest contradiction. For, what are the fore-mentioned objects but the things we perceive by sense? and what do we perceive besides our own ideas or sensations? and is it not plainly repugnant that any one of these, or any combination of them, should exist unperceived?

7. From what has been said it is evident there is not any other substance than *spirit,* or that which perceives. But, for the fuller demonstration of this point, let it be considered [acknowledged that] the sensible qualities are colour, figure, motion, smell, taste, &c., *i.e.,* the ideas perceived by sense. Now, for an idea to exist in an unperceiving thing is a manifest contradiction, for to have an idea is all one as to perceive; that therefore wherein colour, figure, &c. exist must perceive them; hence it is clear there can be no unthinking substance or *substratum* of those ideas.

8. But, say you, though the ideas themselves do not exist without the mind, yet there may be things *like* them, whereof they are copies or resemblances, which things exist without the mind in an unthinking substance. I answer, an idea can be like nothing but an idea; a colour or figure can be like nothing but another colour or figure. If we look but never so little into our own thoughts, we shall find it impossible for us to conceive a likeness except only between our ideas. Again, I ask whether those supposed *originals* or external things, of which our ideas are the pictures or representations, be themselves perceivable

or no? If they are, then *they* are ideas and we have gained our point; but if you say they are not, I appeal to any one whether it be sense to assert a colour is like something which is invisible; hard or soft, like something which is intangible; and so of the rest.

9. Some there are who make a distinction betwixt *primary* and *secondary* qualities. By the former they mean extension, figure, motion, rest, solidity or impenetrability, and number; by the latter they denote all other sensible qualities, as colours, sounds, tastes, and so forth. The ideas we have of these they acknowledge not to be the resemblances of anything existing without the mind, or unperceived, but they will have our ideas of the primary qualities to be patterns or images of things which exist without the mind, in an unthinking substance which they call *matter*. By *matter*, therefore, we are to understand an inert, senseless substance, in which extension, figure, and motion do actually subsist. But it is evident, from what we have already shewn, that extension, figure, and motion are only ideas existing in the mind, and that an idea can be like nothing but another idea, and that consequently neither they nor their archetypes can exist in an unperceiving substance. Hence, it is plain that the very notion of what is called *matter* or *corporeal substance,* involves a contradiction in it.

10. They who assert that figure, motion, and the rest of the primary or original qualities do exist without the mind in unthinking substances, do at the same time acknowledge that colours, sounds, heat, cold, and such like secondary qualities, do not—which they tell us are sensations existing in the mind alone, that depend on and are occasioned by the different size, texture, and motion of the minute particles of matter. This they take for an undoubted truth, which they can demonstrate beyond all exception. Now, if it be certain that those original qualities are inseparably united with the other sensible qualities, and not, even in thought, capable of being abstracted from them, it plainly follows that they exist only in the mind. But I desire any one to reflect and try whether he can, by any abstraction of thought, conceive the extension and motion of a body without all other sensible qualities. For my own part, I see evidently that it is not in my power to frame an idea of a body extended and moving, but I must withal give it some colour or other sensible quality which is acknowledged to exist only in the mind. In short, extension, figure, and motion, abstracted from all other qualities, are inconceivable. Where therefore the other sensible qualities are, there must these be also, to wit, in the mind and nowhere else.

14. I shall farther add, that, after the same manner as modern philosophers prove certain sensible qualities to have no existence in matter, or without the mind, the same thing may be likewise proved of all other sensible qualities whatsoever. Thus, for instance, it is said that heat and cold are affections only of the mind, and not at all patterns of real beings, existing in the corporeal substances which excite them, for [the reason] that the same body which appears cold to one hand seems warm to another. Now, why may we not as well argue that figure and extension are not patterns or resemblances of qualities existing in matter, because to the same eye at different stations, or eyes of a different texture at the same station, they appear various, and cannot therefore be the images of anything settled and determinate without the mind? Again, it is proved that sweetness is not really in the sapid [tasty] thing, because the thing remaining unaltered the sweetness is changed into bitter, as in case of a fever or otherwise vitiated palate. Is it not as reasonable to say that motion is not without the mind, since if the succession of ideas in the mind become

swifter, the motion, it is acknowledged, shall appear slower without any alteration in any external object?

15. In short, let any one consider those arguments which are thought manifestly to prove that colours and tastes exist only in the mind, and he shall find they may with equal force be brought to prove the same thing of extension, figure, and motion. Though it must be confessed this method of arguing does not so much prove that there is no extension or colour in an outward object, as that we do not know by sense which is the true extension or colour of the object. But the arguments foregoing plainly shew it to be impossible that any colour or extension at all, or other sensible quality whatsoever, should exist in an unthinking subject without the mind, or in truth, that there should be any such thing as an outward object.

16. But let us examine a little the received opinion.—It is said extension is a mode or accident [modification or quality] of matter, and that matter is the *substratum* that supports it. Now I desire that you would explain to me what is meant by matter's *supporting* extension. Say you, I have no idea of matter and therefore cannot explain it. I answer, though you have no positive, yet, if you have any meaning at all, you must at least have a relative idea of matter; though you know not what it is, yet you must be supposed to know what relation it bears to accidents, and what is meant by its supporting them. It is evident *support* cannot here be taken in its usual or literal sense—as when we say that pillars support a building; in what sense therefore must it be taken?

17. If we inquire into what the most accurate philosophers declare themselves to mean by *material substance,* we shall find them acknowledge they have no other meaning annexed to those sounds but the idea of being in general, together with the relative notion of its supporting accidents. The general idea of being appeareth to me the most abstract and incomprehensible of all other; and as for its supporting accidents, this, as we have just now observed, cannot be understood in the common sense of those words; it must therefore be taken in some other sense, but what that is they do not explain. So that when I consider the two parts or branches which make the signification of the words *material substance,* I am convinced there is no distinct meaning annexed to them. But why should we trouble ourselves any farther, in discussing this material *substratum* or support of figure and motion, and other sensible qualities? Does it not suppose they have an existence without the mind? And is not this a direct repugnancy [contradiction], and altogether inconceivable?

18. But, though it were possible that solid, figured, movable substances may exist without the mind, corresponding to the ideas we have of bodies, yet how is it possible for us to know this? Either we must know it by sense or by reason. As for our senses, by them we have the knowledge only of our sensations, ideas, or those things that are immediately perceived by sense, call them what you will: but they do not inform us that things exist without the mind, or unperceived, like to those which are perceived. This the materialists themselves acknowledge. It remains therefore that if we have any knowledge at all of external things, it must be by reason, inferring their existence from what is immediately perceived by sense. But what reason can induce us to believe [in] the existence of bodies without the mind, from what we perceive, since the very patrons of matter themselves do not pretend there is any necessary connexion betwixt them and our ideas? I say it is granted on all hands—and what happens in dreams, frenzies, and the like, puts it beyond dispute—that it is possible we might be affected with all the ideas we have now, though there were no bodies existing without, resembling them. Hence, it is evident the

supposition of external bodies is not necessary for the producing our ideas; since it is granted they are produced sometimes, and might be produced always in the same order, we see them in at present, without their concurrence.

19.   But, though we might possibly have all our sensations without them, yet perhaps it may be thought easier to conceive and explain the manner of their production, by supposing external bodies in their likeness rather than otherwise; and so it might be at least probable that there are such things as bodies that excite their ideas in our minds. But neither can this be said; for, though we give the materialists their external bodies, they by their own confession are never the nearer knowing how our ideas are produced; since they own themselves unable to comprehend in what manner body can act upon spirit, or how it is possible it should imprint any idea in the mind. Hence it is evident the production of ideas or sensations in our minds can be no reason why we should suppose matter or corporeal substances, since that is acknowledged to remain equally inexplicable with or without this supposition. If therefore it were possible for bodies to exist without the mind, yet to hold they do so must needs be a very precarious opinion; since it is to suppose, without any reason at all, that God has created innumerable beings that are entirely useless, and serve to no manner of purpose.

20.   In short, if there were external bodies, it is impossible we should ever come to know it; and if there were not, we might have the very same reasons to think there were that we have now. Suppose—what no one can deny possible—an intelligence without the help of external bodies, to be affected with the same train of sensations or ideas that you are, imprinted in the same order and with like vividness in his mind. I ask whether that intelligence hath not all the reason to believe the existence of corporeal substances, represented by his ideas, and exciting them in his mind, that you can possibly have for believing the same thing? Of this there can be no question—which one consideration were enough to make any reasonable person suspect the strength of whatever arguments he may think himself to have, for the existence of bodies without the mind.

22.   I am afraid I have given cause to think I am needlessly prolix in handling this subject. For, to what purpose is it to dilate on that which may be demonstrated with the utmost evidence in a line or two, to anyone that is capable of the least reflexion? It is but looking into your own thoughts, and so trying whether you can conceive it possible for a sound, figure, or motion, or colour to exist without the mind or unperceived. This easy trial may perhaps make you see that what you contend for is a downright contradiction. Insomuch that I am content to put the whole upon this issue:—If you can but conceive it possible for one extended movable substance, or, in general, for any one idea, or anything like an idea, to exist otherwise than in a mind perceiving it, I shall readily give up the cause. And, as for all that compages [company] of external bodies you contend for, I shall grant you its existence, though you cannot either give me any reason why you believe it exists, or assign any use to it when it is supposed to exist. I say, the bare possibility of your opinion's being true shall pass for an argument that it is so.

23.   But, say you, surely there is nothing easier than for me to imagine trees, for instance, in a park, or books existing in a closet, and nobody to perceive them. I answer, you may so, there is no difficulty in it; but what is all this, I beseech you, more than framing in your mind certain ideas which you call books and trees, and at the same time omitting to frame the idea of any one that may perceive them? But do not you yourself perceive or think of them all the

while? This therefore is nothing to the purpose: it only shews you have the power of imagining or forming ideas in your mind: but it does not shew that you can conceive it possible the objects of your thought may exist without the mind. To make out this, it is necessary that you conceive them existing unconceived or unthought of, which is a manifest repugnancy. When we do our utmost to conceive the existence of external bodies, we are all the while only contemplating our own ideas. But the mind, taking no notice of itself, is deluded to think it can and does conceive bodies existing unthought of or without the mind, though at the same time they are apprehended by or exist in itself. A little attention will discover [reveal] to any one the truth and evidence of what is here said, and make it unnecessary to insist on any other proofs against the existence of *material substance.*

24.   It is very obvious, upon the least inquiry into our own thoughts, to know whether it be possible for us to understand what is meant by the *absolute existence of sensible objects in themselves, or without the mind.* To me it is evident those words mark out either a direct contradiction, or else nothing at all. And to convince others of this, I know no readier or fairer way than to entreat they would calmly attend to their own thoughts; and if by this attention the emptiness or repugnancy of those expressions does appear, surely nothing more is requisite for their conviction. It is on this therefore that I insist, to wit, that the absolute existence of unthinking things are words without a meaning, or which include a contradiction. This is what I repeat and inculcate, and earnestly recommend to the attentive thoughts of the reader.

25.   All our ideas, sensations, notions, or the things which we perceive, by whatsoever names they may be distinguished, are visibly inactive—there is nothing of power or agency included in them. So that one idea or object of thought cannot produce or make any alteration in another. To be satisfied of the truth of this, there is nothing else requisite but a bare observation of our ideas. For, since they and every part of them exist only in the mind, it follows that there is nothing in them but what is perceived: but who ever shall attend to his ideas, whether of sense or reflexion, will not perceive in them any power or activity; there is, therefore, no such thing contained in them. A little attention will discover to us that the very being of an idea implies passiveness and inertness in it, insomuch that it is impossible for an idea to do anything, or, strictly speaking, to be the cause of anything: neither can it be the resemblance or pattern of any active being, as is evident from sect. 8. Whence it plainly follows that extension, figure, and motion cannot be the cause of our sensations. To say, therefore, that these are the effects of powers resulting from the configuration, number, motion, and size of corpuscles, must certainly be false.

26.   We perceive a continual succession of ideas; some are anew excited, others are changed or totally disappear. There is therefore some cause of these ideas, whereon they depend, and which produces and changes them. That this cause cannot be any quality, or idea, or combination of ideas, is clear from the preceding section. It must therefore be a substance; but it has been shewn that there is no corporeal or material substance: it remains therefore that the cause of ideas is an incorporeal active substance or spirit.

27.   A spirit is one simple, undivided, active being—as it perceives ideas it is called the *understanding,* and as it produces or otherwise operates about them it is called the *will.* Hence there can be no idea formed of a soul or spirit; for, all ideas whatever, being passive and inert (see sect. 25), cannot represent unto us, by way of images or likeness, that which acts. A little attention will make it plain to any one that to have an idea which shall be *like* that active principle of motion and change of ideas is absolutely impossible. Such is the nature of

spirit, or that which acts, that it cannot be of itself perceived, but only by the effects which it produceth. If any man shall doubt of the truth of what is here delivered, let him but reflect and try if he can frame the idea of any power or active being; and whether he has ideas of two principal powers, marked by the names *will* and *understanding,* distinct from each other, as well as from a third idea of substance or being in general, with a relative notion of its supporting or being the subject of the aforesaid powers—which is signified by the name *soul* or *spirit.* This is what some hold; but, so far as I can see, the words *will, soul, spirit,* do not stand for different ideas, or, in truth, for any idea at all, but for something which is very different from ideas, and which, being an agent, cannot be like unto, or represented by, any idea whatsoever. Though it must be owned at the same time that we have some *notion* of soul, spirit, and the operations of the mind; such as willing, loving, hating—inasmuch as we know or understand the meaning of these words.

28. I find I can excite ideas in my mind at pleasure, and vary and shift the scene as oft as I think fit. It is no more than willing, and straightway this or that idea arises in my fancy: and by the same power it is obliterated and makes way for another. This making and unmaking of ideas doth very properly denominate the mind active. Thus much is certain and grounded on experience: but when we talk of unthinking agents or of exciting ideas exclusive of volition, we only amuse ourselves with words.

29. But, whatever power I may have over my own thoughts, I find the ideas actually perceived by sense have not a like dependence on my will. When in broad daylight I open my eyes, it is not in my power to choose whether I shall see or no, or to determine what particular objects shall present themselves to my view; and so likewise as to the hearing and other senses; the ideas imprinted on them are not creatures of my will. There is therefore some *other* will or spirit that produces them.

30. The ideas of sense are more strong, lively, and distinct than those of the imagination; they have likewise a steadiness, order, and coherence, and are not excited at random, as those which are the effects of human wills often are, but in a regular train or series—the admirable connexion whereof sufficiently testifies the wisdom and benevolence of its Author. Now the set rules or established methods wherein the Mind we depend on excites in us the ideas of sense, are called the *laws of nature;* and these we learn by experience, which teaches us that such and such ideas are attended with such and such other ideas, in the ordinary course of things.

31. This gives us a sort of foresight which enables us to regulate our actions for the benefit of life. And without this we should be eternally at a loss; we could not know how to act [do] anything that might procure us the least pleasure, or remove the least pain of sense. That food nourishes, sleep refreshes, and fire warms us; that to sow in the seed-time is the way to reap in the harvest; and in general that to obtain such or such ends, such or such means are conducive—all this we know, not by discovering any necessary connexion between our ideas, but only by the observation of the settled laws of nature, without which we should be all in uncertainty and confusion, and a grown man no more know how to manage himself in the affairs of life than an infant just born.

32. And yet this consistent uniform working, which so evidently displays the goodness and wisdom of that Governing Spirit whose will constitutes the laws of nature, is so far from leading our thoughts to him, that it rather sends them wandering after second[ary] causes. For, when we perceive certain ideas of sense constantly followed by other ideas, and we know this is not of our own

doing, we forthwith attribute power and agency to the ideas themselves, and make one the cause of another, than which nothing can be more absurd and unintelligible. Thus, for example, having observed that when we perceive by sight a certain round, luminous figure we at the same time perceive by touch the idea or sensation called heat, we do from thence conclude the sun to be the cause of heat. And in like manner perceiving the motion and collision of bodies to be attended with sound, we are inclined to think the latter the effect of the former.

33. The ideas imprinted on the senses by the Author of nature are called *real things:* and those excited by the imagination being less regular, vivid, and constant, are more properly termed *ideas,* or *images of things,* which they copy and represent. But then our sensations, be they never so vivid and distinct, are nevertheless ideas, that is, they exist in the mind, or are perceived by it, as truly as the ideas of its own framing. The ideas of sense are allowed to have more reality in them, that is to be more strong, orderly, and coherent than the creatures of the mind; but this is no argument that they exist without the mind. They are also less dependent on the spirit, or thinking substance which perceives them, in that they are excited by the will of another and more powerful spirit; yet still they are *ideas,* and certainly no *idea,* whether faint or strong, can exist otherwise than in a mind perceiving it.

FOR FURTHER READING

GEORGE BERKELEY, *Three Dialogues Between Hylas and Philonous, In Opposition to Skeptics & Atheists* (1713). Several editions. Here, especially in Part Three, Berkeley tries to answer all of the objections that might be raised against his position.

GEORGE BERKELEY, *A Treatise Concerning The Principles of Human Knowledge: Wherein the chief causes of error & difficulty in the sciences, with the grounds of skepticism, atheism, and irreligion, are inquired into* (1710). Several editions. Consists of an important introduction, dealing with language, and a Part One with 156 sections (fewer than a quarter of which were reprinted above). Berkeley is said to have lost the manuscript of Part Two.

JONATHAN DANCY, *Berkeley: An Introduction.* Oxford: Blackwell, 1987. Written to introduce relatively inexperienced readers to Berkeley's philosophy and its relevance to contemporary philosophical debates.

J. O. URMSON, *Berkeley.* Oxford: Oxford University Press, 1982. A very short and sympathetic overview of Berkeley's thought.

G. J. WARNOCK, *Berkeley.* London: Penguin, 1953. An interesting critical analysis written from the viewpoint of "ordinary language philosophy."

O. K. BOUWSMA, "Notes on Berkeley's Idealism," in *Toward a New Sensibility.* Lincoln, Nebraska: University of Nebraska Press, 1982. A trenchant and entertainingly-written analysis of the "exceedingly interesting compound of confusions" to be found in Berkeley's *Principles,* Sections 3 and 4.

GODFREY VESEY, ed., *Philosophy in the Open.* Milton Keynes, England: The Open University Press, 1974. See Chapter One, "Hylas Fights Back."

QUESTIONS

1. Summarize Berkeley's philosophy in one or two sentences.

2. State and discuss some of Berkeley's arguments for metaphysical idealism.

3.   State and discuss Berkeley's arguments for epistemological idealism.

4.   Compare Berkeley's position with (a) direct realism, and (b) representational realism. (Review the Introduction.)

5.   Summarize and assess Berkeley's critique of Locke's distinction between primary and secondary qualities.

6.   Berkeley argues that the words "material substance" make no sense. What is his argument, and why doesn't he think that the same line of argument applies to the words "spiritual substance"?

7.   In Sections 22–24 of the *Principles,* Berkeley argues that one cannot even conceive it possible that the objects of one's thoughts may exist without (independent of) the mind. What is his premise? Does his conclusion follow necessarily from his premise? (Suggestion: Concentrate on Sec. 23.)

8.   Is there any similarity between the God of Berkeley's *Principles* and the Evil Genius of Descartes' First Meditation? (See Sec. 20 of the *Principles.*)

9.   Why doesn't Berkeley think that one idea could ever produce or alter another idea?

10.   Can we have any *idea* of God, or of any other spirit (mind), in Berkeley's sense of "idea"? How does Berkeley arrive at knowledge of the existence of God?

11.   How does Berkeley distinguish "ideas of sense" from "ideas of imagination"? (See *Principles,* Sec. 33.)

12.   Upon hearing about Berkeley's idealist philosophy, the great eighteenth-century literary personage, Dr. Samuel Johnson, is said to have reacted by "striking his foot with mighty force against a large stone" and saying, "I refute it thus." Evaluate this famous "refutation." (Optional: Sum up and assess O.K. Bouwsma's notes on Johnson's "refutation by kicking." See For Further Reading.)

13.   Discuss: "We can *imagine* a game in which 'Such and such a body is there' is short for 'I have had such and such impressions.' But to take this as the general rule is to simplify our language—to construct a [language] game which is not the one actually played" (Ludwig Wittgenstein, "Cause and Effect," *Philosophia,* Vol. 6 [1976], p. 440).

NOTES

[1]Colin M. Turbane, ed., *Three Dialogues* (Indianapolis: Bobbs-Merrill, 1954), p. 58.
[2]Compare with Locke's "Of Power," pp. 62–64, above.
[3]I am indebted in this section to Urmson and Warnock (see For Further Reading).

chapter 6

HUME

SKEPTICAL EMPIRICISM

David Hume (1711–1776), brought up in the Calvinist Church of his native
Scotland, rejected Christianity in his teens and maintained a thoroughly
secular attitude throughout the rest of his life. The efforts of earlier philosophers—Berkeley, Locke, Leibniz, Descartes, and the medieval Scholastics—
to reconcile natural human understanding with biblical religious faith
seemed to him thoroughly misguided. For he was convinced that such faith
actually *subverts* the foundations of human understanding.

During his lifetime, Hume was esteemed more for his historical works
(especially his monumental *History of England*) than for his strictly philosophical treatises, which constitute the basis for his present-day reputation and
influence. His major philosophical works include:

> *A Treatise of Human Nature, Being an Attempt to Introduce the Experimental Method
> of Reasoning into Moral Subjects* (1739–1740)
>
> *An Enquiry Concerning Human Understanding* (1748)
>
> *An Enquiry Concerning the Principles of Morals* (1751)
>
> *Four Dissertations* (1757): *Natural History of Religion, Of the Passions, Of Tragedy,
> Of the Standard of Taste*
>
> *Dialogues Concerning Natural Religion* (1779)

In the first *Enquiry*, as in the earlier *Treatise,* Hume carried on, and deepened, the investigation of the nature and limits of human understanding that had been initiated by Locke. Like Locke, he worked from the empiricist principle that all the materials of knowledge come from sense experience, rejecting the rationalist search for a supersensible (or transcendent) source of knowledge. But the conclusions he drew from this principle were more skeptical than those of Locke.

Descartes had attempted to give human understanding a rational foundation—a basis in the clear and distinct perception of relations between ideas. Hume argued (and here he went much further than Locke) that human understanding is constituted by a number of basic certainties—about the external world, the future, and causes—and that these certainties are "a species of natural instincts, which no reasoning or process of thought and understanding is able either to produce or to prevent" (*EHU*, p. 30).[1]

We shall study the *Enquiry Concerning Human Understanding,* a shortened and more readable version of the epistemology of the *Treatise,* and the *Dialogues Concerning Natural Religion,* a literary masterpiece and a classic in the philosophy of religion. In both works, Hume developed the critique of rationalism and the analysis of "experimental (empirical) reasoning" which are his major contributions to philosophy.

As they are best read in full, and as they are too long to reprint here, students will have to obtain copies of the *Enquiry* and the *Dialogues* for themselves. The commentaries that follow are meant to be read in conjunction with those volumes.

COMMENTS ON *AN ENQUIRY CONCERNING HUMAN UNDERSTANDING*

The Origin of Ideas (Sec. II)

The materials of human understanding, "the perceptions of the mind," are distinguished by their different degrees of force and vivacity. "The less forcible and lively are commonly denominated *thoughts* or *ideas* ... By the term *impression* ... I mean all our more lively perceptions, when we hear, or see, or feel, or love, or hate, or desire, or will" (p. 10). Notice that the preceding list includes impressions that arise from reflection on our own mind, as well as sense impressions.

The creative power of the mind is limited to the ability to compound, transpose, augment, or diminish the materials afforded us by sensation and reflection. The mind is able to construct *compound ideas* of things that we have not seen or felt (e.g., golden mountains, God) out of *simple ideas,* which are images of things that we have seen or felt (e.g., yellowness, intelligence).

The "airy" speculations of the rationalists resulted from their failure to acknowledge that our ideas must be derived from what we can experience. They postulated very abstract, innate ideas, which were supposed to be clearer and more distinct than any ideas derived from sensation or feeling. But, says Hume, "all ideas, especially abstract ones, are naturally faint and obscure" (p. 13).

Now, since the meanings of words are the ideas for which they stand, words that stand for no ideas at all are mere meaningless marks:

> When we entertain . . . any suspicion that a philosophical term is employed without any meaning or idea (as is but too frequent), we need but enquire, *from what impression is that supposed idea derived?* And if it be impossible to assign any, this will serve to confirm our suspicion. (p. 13)

The abstruse philosophy of the rationalists fails, in Hume's judgment, to pass this test of meaningfulness. In trying to separate thought from feeling, ideas from impressions, the rationalists produced metaphysical jargon rather than significant discourse.

The following passage from the *Treatise* provides a nice illustration of Hume's employment of his principle of meaningfulness:

> . . . [W]hen I enter most intimately into what I call *myself,* I always stumble on some particular perception or other, of heat or cold, light or shade, love or hatred, pain or pleasure. I never can catch *myself* at any time without a perception, and never can observe anything but the perception. (*Treatise:* I, iv, 6)

In other words, Hume is unable to find an impression corresponding to the term "thinking substance," a term which philosophers from Descartes to Berkeley had supposed to signify *the self,* as a permanent subject underlying changing perceptions. So he rejects this term as meaningless, concluding that the words *self* and *mind* can signify "nothing but a bundle or collection of different perceptions which succeed each other with an inconceivable rapidity and are in a perpetual flux and movement" (*Treatise:* I, iv, 6).

In Section VII of the *Enquiry,* Hume subjects the idea of necessary connection to the same sort of scrutiny.

The Association of Ideas (Sec. III)

Human thought is furnished with a great and ever-changing multiplicity of ideas. But, although separate and distinct, these ideas are somehow linked in thought, so that they form together a cosmos rather than a chaos. Because they introduce themselves with a certain degree of method and regularity, it is evident that they are linked according to certain principles, which are "really *to us* the cement of the universe."[2]

These principles, or *laws of association,* are three in number:

1. *Resemblance.* The idea of one object tends to call to mind ideas of resembling objects. We are thereby enabled to classify things, bringing many resembling ideas under one heading.

2. *Contiguity in time or place.* When the Civil War is mentioned, we tend to think of Lincoln, or of others who lived at that time; when the U.S. Capitol is mentioned, it naturally makes us think of Washington, D.C., and of other buildings in that place.

3. *Cause and effect.* The idea of a fresh egg falling to the ground calls to mind the idea of a splattered mess. (Hume considers this the most puzzling of the three principles. He discusses it in the next two sections, and in the seventh.)

Although the mind has no innate *ideas,* it does have an innate *tendency* to organize the ideas presented to it in accordance with these three principles. This tendency is what enables us to think or reason—that is, to collect our ideas into thoughts or (to use an equivalent expression) propositions.

Skeptical Doubts About Empirical Reasoning (Sec. IV)

Human understanding is furnished with a faculty of perception and a faculty of reason. The objects of perception are, as we have seen, impressions and ideas. The objects of reason are propositions. Propositions are either *a priori* statements about relations of ideas or *empirical* statements about matters of fact and real existence.

Relations of ideas can be known either intuitively (e.g., every right triangle has an hypotenuse) or demonstratively (e.g., the square of the hypotenuse is equal to the sum of the squares on the other two sides). Such propositions are *a priori,* i.e., their truth is discoverable without empirical inquiry into what is anywhere existent in the universe. They are also *analytic* (to use a Kantian[3] term), i.e., they cannot be denied without contradiction.

A *matter-of-fact* proposition is never analytic: "The contrary of every matter of fact is still possible; because it can never imply a contradiction. ..." (p. 15). Its truth or falsehood cannot, therefore, be ascertained by the mere analysis of ideas: it must be ascertained empirically (*a posteriori*).

What is the nature of the empirical evidence which assures us of any real existence or matter of fact? We are assured of some facts by the present testimony of our senses or the records of our memory. But by what means do we get beyond such facts? This, the central question of the *Enquiry,* is answered as follows: It is by means of the relation of *cause and effect* that we are enabled to make (more or less reasonable) predictions and conjectures that go beyond the data of perception and memory.

> ... [I]t is constantly supposed that there is a connection between the present fact and that which is inferred from it. Were there nothing to bind them together, the inference would be entirely precarious. The hearing of an articulate voice and rational discourse in the dark assures us of the presence of some person: Why? Because these are the *effects* of the human make and fabric, and closely connected with it. (pp. 16–17, my emphasis)

But how do we arrive at the knowledge of cause and effect? Not by reasoning *a priori,* but "entirely from experience, when we find, that any particular objects are constantly conjoined with each other" (p. 17).

What is the foundation of all conclusions from experience? Such arguments (inductive arguments, as they're called nowadays) have the form: I have found that such an object has been attended with such an effect; therefore, other objects which are in appearance similar will be attended with similar effects. Thus, as Hume phrased it in his *Abstract of A Treatise of Human Nature:* "All reasonings from experience are founded on the supposition that the course of nature will continue uniformly the same."

Does this supposition have any rational foundation? All reasoning is either demonstrative (abstract reasoning *a priori*) or probable (inductive). But there are no demonstrative arguments in the case (i.e., arguments with analytic conclusions), for it implies no contradiction to say that the course of nature may change. "If we be, therefore, engaged by arguments to put trust in past experience and make it the standard of our future judgment, these arguments must be probable only, or such as regard matter of fact and real existence. . . ." (p. 22). But, since all such arguments proceed upon the supposition that the future will be conformable to the past, endeavoring to prove this supposition by probable arguments is arguing in a circle. In other words, the judgment that experience is a valid ground of judgments cannot itself be grounded in experience.[4]

Skeptical Solution of These Doubts (Sec. V)

The conclusion of the previous section was that there is no way to prove that we really have knowledge of any matter of fact beyond the present testimony of our senses or the records of our memory: " . . . in all reasonings from experience there is a step taken by the mind which is not supported by any argument or process of the understanding" (p. 27). In this section Hume argues that "if the mind be not engaged by argument to make this step, it must be induced by some other principle of equal weight and authority" (p. 27). That principle is a certain natural instinct called *custom* or *habit:*

> . . . [A]fter the constant conjunction of two objects, heat and flame, for instance . . . we are determined by custom alone to expect the one from the appearance of the other. (p. 28) It is that principle alone which renders our experience useful to us. . . . Without the influence of custom, we should be entirely ignorant of every matter of fact, beyond what is immediately present to the memory and senses. We should never know how to adjust means to ends, or to employ our natural powers in the production of any effect. There would be an end at once of all action, as well as of the chief part of speculation. (p. 29)

Although we must admit, *in theory,* that this "custom," like any other human instinct, may be deceitful, *in practice* we cannot help believing in it.

In his Fourth Meditation, Descartes had claimed that belief is totally under our voluntary control. Against this voluntaristic theory of belief, Hume points out, in Part II of this section, that

We can, in our conception, join the head of a man to the body of a horse; but it is not in our power to believe that such an animal has ever really existed. (p. 31)

"Belief," says Hume, "is nothing but a more vivid, lively, forcible, firm, steady conception of an object, than what the imagination alone is ever able to attain" (p. 32). And he explains its origins as follows: "After the constant conjunction of two objects, heat and flame, for instance, we are determined by custom to expect the one from the appearance of the other." That is, we are determined to *believe* that fire is hot and to act accordingly. It is not within our power to suspend judgment in such a case; for here belief is something that *happens* to us, not something we arrive at by active ratiocination.

Probability (Sec. VI)

Basing his argument on everyday linguistic usage, Hume criticizes Locke's view that whenever an argument is not demonstrative (abstract and *a priori*, as in mathematics) then it is, at best, merely probable:

In this view, we must say that it is only probable all men must die, or that the sun will rise tomorrow. But to conform our language more to common use, we ought to divide arguments into *demonstrations, proofs,* and *probabilities.* By proofs meaning such arguments from experience as leave no room for doubt or opposition. (p. 37, footnote)

Hume's view, as expressed in this section (and later, in Sec. X, "Of Miracles") is that inductive arguments prove their conclusions when they are based on "entirely regular and uniform" experience (p. 38). Such arguments, since they "leave no room for any contrary supposition" (p. 38), are not subject to reasonable doubt. It would be therefore improper and misleading to call them merely probable arguments.

The skeptic about the operations of the human understanding, in Section IV, wanted to cast doubt on *all* inductive inferences, even those based on entirely regular and uniform experience. In Section V, Hume maintained that the only remedy against such skepticism is immersion in the affairs of common life and practice, where it will be found that reliance on inductive proof is irresistible and indispensable. In the present section, Hume seems to imply that the skeptic's doubts do not, in everyday language and common use, count as *reasonable doubts* at all.[5]

The Idea of Necessary Connection (Sec. VII)

Although knowledge of cause and effect comes only by way of experience,

> ... experience only teaches us how one event constantly follows another, without instructing us in the secret connection which binds them together and renders them inseparable. (p. 43)

But Locke imagined that if we could only perceive the minute structure of substances, then we would be able to infer *a priori* what their properties must be. For example, if we could only clearly and distinctly perceive the minute structure of water, we would understand why it must freeze when cooled to 0°C, just as we now understand why the square on the hypotenuse of a right triangle must equal the sum of the squares on its other two sides. Hume denies this, pointing out that no matter-of-fact proposition is necessary in the sense in which a mathematical proposition is necessary. The denial of the Pythagorean theorem entails a contradiction; the denial of the proposition that water freezes at 0°C is, as a matter of fact, false, but it entails no contradiction.

Descartes had argued that in a human being certain physical events *cause* certain conscious states. Some of his earliest critics had objected that there is no intelligible (i.e., logical or mathematical) connection between a physical (extended) event and a mental (nonextended) state. Now Hume agreed that there is no intelligible connection but denied that this is a valid objection to Descartes' theory. He argued that causal theories are *never* based on the perception of an intelligible connection between events.

Berkeley thought that we got our idea of causation by reflecting on the voluntary operations of the mind. He asserted, Hume notes,

> ... that we are conscious of power or energy in our minds when, by an act or command of our will, we raise up a new idea.... (p. 44)

Hume objects that we

> ... only feel the event, namely, the existence of an idea, consequent to the command of the will: but the manner in which this operation is performed, the power by which it is produced, is entirely beyond our comprehension. (p. 45)

Having been unable to find an origin for the idea of necessary connection in either impressions of sensation or impressions of reflection, Hume is tempted to excise the phrases "causal connection" and "causal power" from his vocabulary:

> All events seem entirely loose and separate. One event follows another; but we never can observe any tie between them. They seem *conjoined* but never *connected*. And as we can have no idea of any thing which never appeared to our outward sense or inward sentiment, the necessary conclusion *seems* to be that we have no idea of connection or power at all, and that these words

are absolutely without any meaning, when employed either in philosophical reasoning or in common life. (p. 49)

Hume does indeed reject the word "connection" as it was employed in remote metaphysical reasonings. But he does not reject its everyday or common employment. For he finally discovers, in common life and practice, and experimental (experiential) origin for the idea of necessary connection. But the origin of the idea turns out to be quite different from what we had expected:

> ... [A]fter a repetition of similar instances the mind is carried by habit, upon the appearance of one event, to expect its usual attendant, and to believe that it will exist. This connection, therefore, which we *feel* in the mind, this customary [conditioned] transition of the imagination from one object to its usual attendant, is the sentiment or impression from which we form the idea of power or necessary connection.... (p. 50)

We say that dropping an egg will cause it to break. If asked why we believe this, we may claim that we just *see* that there's a connection between the two sorts of events such that if the one occurs, the other is bound to follow. And we may imagine that our *criterion* for judging that the dropping will cause the breaking is the perception of a necessary connection between the two sorts of events. In fact, however, we judge as we do only because of past experience: We have frequently observed the one sort of event following upon the other, and we have gotten into the habit of expecting the one upon the appearance of the other. The truth is that the mind *attributes* a necessary connection to the two events because of past perception of constant conjunction; it does not judge that the two events are causally related because it has *discovered* a necessary connection between them:

> The first time a man saw the communication of motion by impulse, as by the shock of two billiard-balls, he could not pronounce that the one event was *connected,* but only that it was *conjoined* with the other. After he has observed several instances of this nature, he then pronounces them to be *connected.* What alteration has happened to give rise to this new idea of *connection?* Nothing but that he now *feels* these events to be *connected* in his imagination, and can readily foretell the existence of one from the appearance of the other. When we say, therefore, that one object is connected with another, we mean only that they have acquired a connection in our thought, and give rise to the inference by which they become proofs of each other's existence.... (pp. 50–51)

In other words: We do not make a causal inference because we perceive a connection between events; we "perceive a connection between events" because we make causal inferences. This "perceived connection" is really a *fiction* generated by the imagination in accordance with the laws of association.

Liberty and Necessity (Sec. VIII)

The dilemma of freedom and determinism (or of liberty and necessity, as Hume calls it) is as follows: If our actions are caused, then they are necessitated; but if they are necessitated, they are not free, and therefore not properly subject to moral praise or blame. So it seems that we must either deny causality, thus giving up the application of experimental reason to moral subjects, or else deny freedom, thereby subverting the moral and political institutions which presuppose it.

Hume argues that this dilemma arises from unclarity about the ideas of necessity and liberty.

In Section II, he maintained that ideas are to be clarified by tracing them back to the impressions from which they originated. In the preceding section, he traced the idea of necessary connection to the mind's natural reaction to impressions of constant conjunction:

> Beyond the constant *conjunction* of similar objects, and the consequent *inference* from one to the other, we have no notion of any necessity, or connection. (p. 55)

And this notion, as Hume shows with many examples in the present section, applies to human behavior, as much as to anything else:

> ... The conjunction between motives and voluntary actions is as regular and uniform, as that between the cause and effect in any part of nature, [and] ... this experienced uniformity in human actions is a source, whence we draw *inferences* concerning them. (p. 59)

So there is no sense in which natural processes are caused or necessitated, but voluntary behavior is not. What, then, is the difference between them?

A voluntary action is a movement caused by the *will* of the agent. And the origin of the idea of the will is certain impressions of reflection, namely: passions, sentiments, desires. We feel that agents are subject to moral judgment to the extent that we regard their actions as springing from their own passions, sentiments, or desires:

> For as actions are objects of our moral sentiment, so far only as they are indications of the internal character, passions, and affections; it is impossible that they can give rise either to praise or blame, where they proceed not from these principles, but are derived altogether from external violence. (p. 66)

Just as the attribution of causality is rooted in the natural disposition to expect for the future the sort of conjunctions observed in the past, so the attribution of moral responsibility is rooted in the natural disposition to praise or blame voluntary actions:

> The mind of a man is so formed by nature, that, upon the appearance of certain characters, dispositions, and actions, it immediately feels the sentiment of approbation or blame. . . . [The distinction between virtue and vice is] founded in the natural sentiments of the human mind: And these sentiments are not to be controlled or altered by any philosophical theory or speculation whatsoever.[6] (p. 68)

Where some philosophers had thought it necessary to *justify* (or to alter) these "natural sentiments of the human mind," Hume contented himself with *describing* them and the circumstances in which they actually operate.

Our moral sentiments operate when we judge an action free, and we judge it free when we judge it to flow from a certain *liberty* in the agent. But:

> By liberty . . . we can only mean *a power of acting or not acting, according to the determinations of the will;* that is, if we choose to remain at rest, we may; if we choose to move, we also may. Now this hypothetical liberty is universally allowed to belong to every one, who is not a prisoner and in chains. Here then is no subject of dispute. (p. 63)

So when we speak of a human action as *free* we are saying that it was not caused *in a certain way* (by constraint or external violence), but we are not saying that it was uncaused absolutely. Indeed, when we praise or blame an individual for his or her behavior, we *must* believe that it was caused. For where actions

> . . . proceed not from some *cause* in the character and disposition [the will] of the person who performed them, they can neither redound to his honor, if good; nor infamy, if evil. (p. 65)

It is a universally allowed maxim of experimental reasoning that every event has a cause. But we are tempted by a certain false sensation or seeming experience to imagine that our own free actions are an exception to this maxim, and to attribute to them an absolute liberty—a freedom from any sort of necessitation. For in performing actions we feel that they are

> . . . subject to our will, on most occasions; and imagine [that] we feel that the will itself is subject to nothing, because, when by a denial of it we are provoked to try, we feel that it moves easily every way, and produces an image of itself . . . even on that side on which it did not settle. This image, or faint motion, we persuade ourselves, could at that time, have been completed into the thing itself; because, should that be denied, we find, upon a second trial, that at present it can. We consider not that the fantastical desire of showing liberty is here the motive of our actions. (p. 63, footnote)

So experience does not really teach us that our will is itself subject to nothing; it teaches us only that, on many occasions, *if* we had willed otherwise, *then* we could have acted otherwise than we actually did. "And it seems certain," Hume continues, "that however [much] we may imagine we feel an [absolute] liberty within ourselves, a spectator can commonly infer our actions from our motives and character; and even where he cannot, he concludes in general that he might, were he perfectly acquainted with every circumstance of our situation and temper.... Now this is the very essence of necessity, according to the foregoing doctrine" (p. 63, footnote).

In sum: Once we clarify the ideas of necessity and liberty, by tracing them to their real origins in experience, we find that there is no contradiction in the belief that an action can be both morally free and causally necessitated.[7]

The Reason of Animals (Sec. IX)

In spite of their obvious differences, Hume and Spinoza were alike in one very important respect: They shared a thoroughly *naturalistic*[8] view of things. And thus both, each in his own way, tended to emphasize the continuity between humanity and the rest of nature.

This naturalistic—and very modern—viewpoint finds clear expression in the present section.

Hume observes that animals make inferences to facts beyond what immediately strike their senses, and that it

> ... is impossible that this inference of the animal can be founded on any process of argument or reasoning by which he concludes that like events must follow like objects, and that the course of nature will always be regular in its operation. (p. 70)

The same applies to children and to adults in their ordinary actions and conclusions. "An operation of such immense consequence in life, as that of inferring effects from causes, [cannot] be trusted to the uncertain processes of reason and argumentation" (p. 71).

It is true that some humans surpass all animals in experimental reasoning. This is due, in part, to the fact that human beings alone have developed an art of controlled experiment: "The circumstance on which the effect depends is frequently involved in other circumstances which are foreign and extrinsic. The separation of it often requires great attention, accuracy, and subtlety" (p. 71, footnote). But this art is merely a refinement of a power which we possess in common with beasts.

Neither animals nor human beings reason with themselves in the following way: "Fire has always burned me in the past, so it will probably burn me on this occasion as well." As the twentieth-century Austrian philosopher Ludwig Wittgenstein put it:

The squirrel does not infer by induction that it is going to need stores next winter as well. And no more do we need a law of induction to justify our actions or predictions. But that means I want to conceive [this certainty] as something that lies beyond being justified or unjustified; as it were, as something animal.[9]

The belief that fire will burn me is of the same kind as the fear that it will burn me.[10]

Belief is here something that happens to us—a passion or reaction, rather than a reasoned conclusion. And this *natural* reaction to fire, for example, is more basic than any *reasoned* belief we may have about it.[11]

Miracles (Sec. X)

Is there any basis in reason or evidence for accepting doctrines of a "revealed religion," such as Christianity? Many Christians say that they accept their religion because it is divinely revealed—"because God vouches for it." And many apologists for the Christian religion have appealed to the miracles reported in the Bible in support of the claim to divine revelation, arguing that Jesus did certain things to show that his teachings were backed up by supernatural power and authority.

Hume's attack on the preceding rationale for religious faith is among the more provocative parts of his philosophy. He contends that it is never reasonable to believe the report of a miracle, since (1) a miracle would be a glaringly improbable event, one contrary to past experience and experimental reasoning, and (2) no testimonial evidence could ever outweigh the inherent improbability of a story reporting such an event. Using a number of subsidiary arguments and vivid concrete illustrations, Hume develops this case powerfully in the present section. The reader is urged to study it carefully.

At the end of the section Hume tells us, in effect, that Christians ought to give up apologetic efforts to make their religion sound reasonable. For their religion is based on *faith*—a faith which "subverts all the principles of [a person's] understanding, and gives him a determination to believe what is most contrary to custom and experience" (p. 90).

John Locke, a guiding spirit of the Enlightenment, had argued for the supremacy of reason over faith:

Reason must be our last judge and guide in everything. I do not mean that we must consult reason, and examine whether a proposition revealed by God can be made out by natural principles, and if it cannot, that then we may reject it: but consult it we must, and by it examine, whether it be a revelation from God or not. . . . (*Essay:* IV, xix, 14)

He had also, in his *Reasonableness of Christianity* (1695) and elsewhere, defended a version of Christian faith as being more reasonable than any competing faith, making extensive use of the argument from (Gospel) miracles to that end. But, according to Hume, Locke's argument misrepresents the true character of the faith and "puts it to a trial which it is by no means fitted to endure." For, in Hume's view, faith has no foundation in reason and is even contrary to it (a view that was to be taken up by a philosopher much more sympathetic to Christianity, Søren Kierkegaard, in the nineteenth century).

As an appendix to this section, I quote a short editorial discussion of the famous Israeli psychic, Uri Geller.[12] As this editorial makes clear, Hume's argument in this section of the *Enquiry* is applicable in philosophy of science as well as in philosophy of religion.

Uri Geller

Public curiosity is much wider than the range of practical and moral issues, and the bearing of philosophy on matters of public opinion accordingly extends to abstract and theoretical questions. In recent months the theory of knowledge has been discussed almost daily in the press and on radio and television in connection with the feats of Mr. Uri Geller. A Professor of Psychology who refused to watch the television programme in which Mr. Geller bent spoons by will-power has been compared to the Cardinals who refused to look through Galileo's telescope. He could defend himself by a judicious use of Hume's argument against miracles. The argument uses a principle that every man uses every day in his ordinary affairs: the principle that the antecedent certainty of a conclusion may be so great as to amount to a good reason for rejecting an argument that purports to overturn that conclusion. Of course mistakes can be made in the application of this as of any other principle; and the Cardinals were undoubtedly wrong in their conclusion. But it does not follow that they were being irrational or even unreasonable in the light of the evidence available to them. The oriental potentate described by Edgar Allen Poe had good reason for refusing to believe in steam engines or in ice and snow. At least until Stanford University or some other authority can furnish further and better particulars than have so far been published, that is where the matter stands. It is certain that feats more amazing than those performed by Mr. Geller are performed daily and nightly at children's parties and variety theatres. As Hume said, we must proportion our belief to the evidence, and nobody who does that can persuade himself at this stage that Mr. Uri Geller has any power not available to Mr. David Nixon [a British illusionist].

The progress of science requires skepticism about surprising claims quite as much as it requires open-mindedness to new ideas. The two requirements will naturally often appear to conflict, and it will sometimes be made to appear that we have to choose one of them as a permanent posture to the exclusion of the other. That way lies unreason, in one or another of its myriad forms.

Of a Particular Providence
and of a Future State (Sec. XI)

The *Enquiry* is, to a great extent, an examination of experimental rea-soning. The present section concerns the scope and limits of that method of reasoning in natural theology, i.e., in arguments for the existence of God. This topic is discussed at much greater length in the *Dialogues Concerning Natural Religion;* we shall take it up in the context of our study of that work.

Academic Skepticism (Sec. XII)

There are three parts to this complicated concluding section. In the first, Hume distinguishes various species of skepticism and then discusses arguments for skepticism with regard to the senses. In the second, he pre-sents the case for skepticism with regard to both abstract and experimental reasoning. In the third, he defends a species of skepticism, deriving from the Academy of Hellenistic Greece, known as Academic skepticism.

I shall confine my remarks to two topics: (1) the "profound" argument for doubting the senses, contained in Part I, and (2) the "academic" solution to these and similar doubts, contained in Part III.

(1)

Empiricist philosophers take it for granted that we acquire knowledge of the world by way of sense experience. And yet they must face up to the fact that certain arguments, such as the following, lead to the conclusion that what we really perceive is not the *world* (things existing independently of our perception of them) but rather *ideas* (images of things):

> The table which we see seems to diminish as we remove [move back] further from it; but the real table, which exists independent of us, suffers no alter-ation. It was therefore, nothing but its image which was present to the mind. (p. 104)[13]

Therefore there appears to be a gap between the world and our perception of it. And this provokes the skeptical question: How can we possibly know that *any* of our ideas bridge that gap and give knowledge of the world?

Descartes had claimed to prove that some of our ideas are caused by, and resemble, corporeal objects existing independently of the mind. His proof involved an appeal to the veracity of God—that is, an appeal to a transcendent and therefore imperceptible bridge between perceptions in the mind and things in the world. Hume rejected this, along with every other attempt to answer questions of fact through abstract reasoning *a priori:*

It is a question of fact whether the perceptions of the senses be produced by external objects resembling them: How shall this question be determined? By experience surely, as all other questions of a like nature. But here experience is, and must be, entirely silent. The mind has never any thing present to it but the perceptions, and cannot possibly reach any experience of their connection with objects. The supposition of such a connection is, therefore, without any foundation in reasoning. (p. 105)

Berkeley had concluded, using an argument similar to the preceding, that we have no reason to believe in material substances, i.e., in permanent objects which cause, and are represented by, the fleeting perception present to consciousness. However, Berkeley did not regard this conclusion as skeptical in character, i.e., at odds with everyday, common-sense convictions. And it is here that Hume disagrees with him, insisting that an (unreasoned) belief in the continuous and mind-independent existence of bodies is "a point which we must take for granted in all our reasonings" (*Treatise:* I, iv, 2).

Now, if we combine the argument for skepticism about the existence of material bodies with the argument, in Section IV, about experimental reasoning (i.e., about our practice of making inferences about the future based on past experience), we have (Hume thinks) an unanswerable rationale for doubting the truth of any matter-of-fact proposition which purports to tell us about anything over and above the impressions immediately present to consciousness.

(2)

What is the effect of these arguments? Hume tells us that "they admit of no answer and produce no conviction." In other words: Although they cannot be refuted, they cannot be believed either, for they go against a powerful principle of human nature, a principle in accordance with which we live and act—the principle of mental association known as cause and effect. Therefore there is no danger that skeptical arguments might subvert the everyday operations of the human mind. What they teach us is that these operations are founded on something prior to any rational conviction. They also have the effect of teaching a certain modesty about the powers of the human mind, in that they bring to light

> ... The whimsical condition of mankind, who must act and reason and believe; though they are not able, by their most diligent inquiry, to satisfy themselves concerning the foundation of these operations, or to remove the objections which may be raised against them. (p. 111)

Pyrrhonism, one school of ancient Greek skepticism, recommended suspending judgment about anything beyond the immediate data of sensation.

Academic skepticism, another school of ancient philosophy, taught a more moderate position, recommending suspension of judgment only when we are delving into subjects remote from the affairs of common life and experience. Hume adopts this moderate skepticism—a position which subverts the dogmas of rationalist metaphysics and the superstitions of popular religion, without at the same time pretending to undermine reason's instinctive confidence in its ability to achieve knowledge within the sphere of human life and practice.

Reason keeps within its properly modest, human sphere by confining its abstract, purely *a priori* inquiry to the mathematical subjects of quantity and number,[14] and by employing the experimental method of reasoning in all inquiries directed to the knowledge of matters of fact and real existence. (The ontological argument[15] for the existence of God, employed by Descartes and other rationalists, is the prime example of a purely *a priori* inquiry about matter of fact and real existence. As such, it should be "committed to the flames, for it can contain nothing but sophistry and illusion.")

Mathematics (arithmetic, geometry), the *general sciences* (physics, chemistry, political science, etc.), and the *particular sciences* (history, astronomy, geography, etc.) all fall clearly within the bounds of rational inquiry. But the place of *theology* is not so clear: It requires the sort of extensive discussion which Hume proceeded to give in his *Dialogues Concerning Natural Religion.*

COMMENTS ON THE *DIALOGUES CONCERNING NATURAL RELIGION*

Hume's *Dialogues,* products of years of writing and rewriting, were published three years after his death by his nephew. They bear close study, not only as an important document of eighteenth-century Enlightenment but also as an unsurpassed introduction to the philosophy of religion. Although no summary can do them justice, the following notes, beginning with a short outline, may be of value in facilitating analysis of the text.

Prologue ("Pamphilus to Hermippus"): Introduction to the Dialogues' subject and participants.
Part I: Philo's Academic skepticism.
Parts II–VIII: Scrutiny of experimental theism (the argument from design).
Part IX: Scrutiny of *a priori* theism (the rationalistic argument for the existence of God).
Parts X–XI: The problem of evil.
Part XII: True religion versus vulgar superstition.

Prologue and Part I

The subject of the *Dialogues* is *natural religion,* i.e., that part of religious truth knowable to us by our natural human powers without the aid of supernatural revelation. The characters are: *Cleanthes,* an empiricist who confidently applies the experimental method of reasoning to natural religion; *Philo,* an empiricist who is more skeptical than Cleanthes about the scope of experimental reason; and *Demea,* a rationalist who defends the use of abstract reasoning *a priori* in proving the existence of God, but who denies that man can reason to any knowledge of the nature of God.

In the opinion of Pamphilus, the narrator, Cleanthes won the debate. But in the opinion of most students of the *Dialogues,* Philo came out ahead and is the major spokesman for Hume's own philosophy of religion. One indication of this is that, as Hume had defended, in his own voice, the moderate skepticism of the Greek Academics at the end of his first *Enquiry,* so Philo defends that species of skepticism in Part I of the *Dialogues:*

> All skeptics pretend that, if reason be considered in an abstract view, it furnishes invincible arguments against itself, and that we could never retain any conviction or assurance on any subject, were not the skeptical reasonings so refined and subtle that they are not able to counter-poise the more solid and more natural arguments, derived from the senses and experience. But it is evident, whenever our arguments lose this advantage, and run wide of common life, that the most refined skepticism . . . is able to oppose and counterbalance them. The one has no more weight than the other. The mind must remain in suspense between them; and it is that very suspense or balance which is the triumph of skepticism.[16] (p. 8)

When we try to apply our common ("vulgar") methods of reasoning to remote theological questions, then, says Philo, "we are like foreigners in a strange country to whom everything must seem suspicious" (p. 7).

Part II

Demea and Philo maintain that, although the *existence* of a deity is "unquestionable and self-evident," the *nature* of the deity is altogether incomprehensible to human understanding. Philo presents the following arguments:

> Nothing exists without a cause; and the original cause of this universe (whatever it be) we call *God,* and piously ascribe to him every species of perfection. . . . But as all perfection is entirely relative, we ought never to imagine that we comprehend the attributes of this divine Being. . . . He is infinitely superior to our limited view and comprehension, and is more the object of worship in the temple than of disputation in the schools.
>   . . . Our ideas reach no further than our experience: We have no experience of divine attributes and operations: I need not conclude my syllogism: You can draw the inference yourself. (pp. 14–15)

Cleanthes now presents an argument for the comprehensibility of God's nature. It is a version of the "teleological" or "design" argument, an argument which, employed since antiquity, reached its peak of popularity in the eighteenth century.

Cleanthes' formulation of the argument can be set out in the following steps:

1) The world itself and its various parts resemble machines and other contrivances of human art.

2) As machines are made up of parts which are required for the successful functioning of the whole, so also do the parts of the world function for the successful functioning of the whole.

3) But the parts of the machine are designed by the inventor to serve in the successful operation of the machine.

4) There must be a designer of the world, who is the cause of its successful operation. (Like effects have like causes.)

5) And we do know certain characteristics of designers, such as intelligence and power.

Therefore,

6) We know certain characteristics of God, such as enormous intelligence and power.

This is *a posteriori* reasoning—probable reasoning from experience, rather than *a priori* reasoning—demonstrative reasoning from self-evident premises.

Philo agrees that only *a posteriori* reasoning can lead to knowledge about the cause of anything. But he doubts that we have adequate experience on which to base any definite theory about the Cause of the Universe—for the universe is unique and thus unlike any object open to human experience. And consequently, when we speculate about such matters, we

> ... are got into fairy land long ere we have reached the last steps of our theory; and *there* we have no reason to trust our common methods of argument, or to think that our usual analogies and probabilities have any authority. Our line is too short to fathom such immense abysses. (*EHU*, Section VII, p. 48)

Philo develops this criticism in Parts IV–VIII and X–XI of these *Dialogues*.

Part III

In the previous part Philo seemed to question the "datum," or empirical starting point, of Cleanthes' argument—the existence of an analogy between works of *nature* and works of *art*. Cleanthes suspects that Philo couldn't have been sincere in this doubt: "Anybody can see the analogy," he claims, for it is "self-evident and undeniable":

> The anatomy of an animal affords many stronger instances of design than the perusal of [the books of] Livy or Tacitus. . . . Choose, then, your party, Philo . . . assert either that a rational volume is no proof of a rational cause or admit of a similar cause to all the works of nature.
>
> . . . Consider, anatomize the eye, survey its structure and contrivance, and tell me, from your own feeling, if the idea of a contriver does not immediately flow in upon you with a force like that of sensation. (p. 25)

Demea objects to the comparison of nature to a book on the gounds that it leads to the impious presumption that the human mind can comprehend the divine mind:

> When I read a volume, I enter into the mind and intention of the author. . . . But so near an approach we never surely can make to the Deity. His ways are not our ways.
>
> . . . by representing the Deity as so intelligible and comprehensible, and so similar to the human mind, we are guilty of the grossest and most narrow partiality, and make ourselves the model of the whole universe. (pp. 26–27)

Part IV

Two objections are made against Cleanthes' design argument, the first by Demea, the second by Philo.

Demea continues the objection that he had started at the end of the previous dialogue, namely that Cleanthes' reasoning, concluding as it does to a deity similar to the human mind, is impiously anthropomorphic.[17]

Cleanthes responds that, if we deny every analogy between the human and the divine, then everything we say about God will be so many "unmeaning epithets." It is essential, he thinks, to believe that God has a *mind.* But if we insist on God's absolute simplicity, as Demea does, then "God's mind" becomes so very different from the human mind (the only mind of which we have any experience) that it turns out to be an abuse of terms to use the same word in both cases. But then, Cleanthes continues, Demea's position is really a form of atheism; for to avoid atheism we must not only believe in a first cause of the universe, we must also believe that it is an *intelligent* cause, and consequently that it has a mind.

Philo now enters the discussion, presenting the second objection to Cleanthes' reasoning. He poses the question: If an intelligent agent is postulated to explain the order in the world, won't we have to postulate a still higher cause to explain the order of *ideas* in the mind of that intelligent agent?

> But if we stop and go no further, [Philo continues,] why go so far? Why not stop at the material world? How can we satisfy ourselves without going on *ad infinitum?* And, after all, what satisfaction is there in that infinite progression? Let us remember that story of the Indian philosopher and his elephant.[18] It

was never more applicable than to the present subject. If the material world rests upon a similar ideal world, this ideal world must rest upon some other, and so on without end. It were better, therefore, never to look beyond the present material world. By supposing it to contain the principle of its order within itself, we really assert it to be God; and the sooner we arrive at the Divine Being, so much the better. When you go one step beyond the mundane system, you only excite an inquisitive humour which it is impossible ever to satisfy. (p. 31)

Note that if you *do* stop at the "mundane system," and believe it to contain *within itself* the Ultimate Principle of its own order, then you have embraced the philosophical position known as *naturalism*—a position, you will remember, that was also held by Spinoza.

Part V

Philo argues that a person who follows Cleanthes' hypothesis

... is able, perhaps, to assert or conjecture that the universe [at] some time arose from something like design; but beyond that position he cannot ascertain one single circumstance, and is left afterwards to fix every point of his theology by the utmost license of fancy and hypothesis. (p. 37)

Experimental reasoning, he argues, can yield no knowledge of attributes traditionally acribed to God, such as infinity, perfection, unity, and immateriality.[19]

Part VI

Starting here, and continuing through Part VIII, Philo presents various alternatives to Cleanthes' explanation of order in the world. For example: If there is a great analogy between the world and works of art, isn't there just as great an analogy between the world and an *animal*? If so, we could liken the cause of order in the world to the soul (vital principle) of an animal, rather than to the mind of a person.

Experimental reasoning, aiming to find probable explanations for a phenomenon, proceeds according to the rule that one explanation should not be accepted unless other explanations have been considered and shown to be less probable than it. Now, although Philo does not regard his suggested alternatives as more probable than Cleanthes' hypothesis, neither does he think it possible to prove them less probable.

Part VII

In this Part, a supplement to the previous one, Philo remains the chief speaker. His main points are two:

1. There seem to be at least three priniciples of order, in addition to reason: generation, vegetation, and instinct. (These are *biological* principles. Hume mentions *mechanical* principles in other places, e.g., gravitation and impulse.)

2. We don't have the data to establish any system of cosmology. One system will try to account for everything in terms of *one* of the principles mentioned, deriving the other principles from it; another system will favor a different principle, etc. We are simply without data sufficient to decide between them.

Part VIII

Philo presents a modified version of an hypothesis devised by the ancient Greek philosopher Epicurus as another possible alternative to Cleanthes' theory. According to this Epicurean theory, the universe consists of a huge but limited number of eternally moving atoms. In an unlimited time-span these would go through all possible combinations. Some of these combinations turn out to be relatively stable, and one of them is the cosmos in which we now live—a cosmos which happens to have just the right conditions for the development and survival of creatures such as ourselves.

Although he regards it as "not absolutely absurd and improbable" p. 50), Philo denies that we have evidence sufficient to establish it or any other system of the origin of the world. He therefore recommends skepticism.

Part IX

The great modern philosopher following directly after Hume, Immanuel Kant, gave the following useful classification of arguments for the existence of God:

1. *Teleological* arguments (or arguments from design), where the inference is from the "purposiveness" or intelligible order in the world to the existence of an intelligent and powerful designer. (This sort of argument is the main subject of the *Dialogues*.)

2. *Cosmological* arguments, where the inference is from the existence of the world to the necessity of a cause of its existence. (A version of this argument is found in the *Monadology* of Leibniz, Section 36–39. Demea defends a similar version in this Part.)

3. *Ontological* arguments, where the necessary existence of God (as "most real being" or "supreme being") is inferred from the concept of God. (Although this argument originated with the medieval theologian St. Anselm, the version of it that Kant and Hume had in mind came from Descartes.)[20]

The first kind of argument tends to appeal to philosphers of an empiricist bent, the second and third to philosophers of a rationalist bent.

Demea, the spokesman for rationalism in the *Dialogues,* advances a proof that appears to involve both the cosmological and the ontological arguments. Cleanthes and Philo, the representatives of empiricism, join forces to refute Demea's "*a priori* proof."

Cleanthes and Philo share Hume's own epistemological position, the position according to which the only evidence assuring us of any real existence and matter of fact is *experience*, that is, the present testimony of our senses, the records of memory, and the causal ("experimental") reasoning based on the empirically observed regularities of past experience.

In the *Enquiry*, Hume had rejected the ontological argument on the grounds that it makes an invalid inference from a matter of definition (the meaning of "God") to a matter of fact (that a supreme being actually exists). His argument, as stated in the following passage from Section XII, is that *real existence* (as opposed to mere mathematical possibility) cannot be contained in the bare conception (definition) of a thing:

> That the cube root of 64 is equal to the half of 10 is a false proposition, and can never be distinctly conceived. But that CAESAR, or the angel GABRIEL, or any other being [even "the Supreme Being"] never existed, may be a false proposition, but still is perfectly conceivable, and implies no contradiction. The existence, therefore, of any being can only be proved by arguments from its cause or its effect; and these arguments are founded entirely on experience. (p. 113)

In the *Critique of Pure Reason* (1781), Kant criticized the ontological argument on similar gounds and criticized the cosmological argument on the grounds that, in the final analysis, it falls into the same error as the ontological. Now it seems to me that his criticisms apply to the "*a priori* proof" of Demea in this Dialogue and that they were anticipated by Cleanthes in his rebuttal of Demea's argument.

Demea reasons as follows: In explaining the existence of anything by appealing to the existence of a *contingent* cause (i.e., a cause which *does not exist by its own intrinsic nature*), you've just pushed back the problem a little further—you have not explained why *anything at all* exists. But there must be an explanation (or cause) of the existence of anything that exists, and thus an explanation of the fact that anything at all exists. Therefore, since something *does* exist, the ultimate explanation for its existence must be some *necessarily* existent cause, i.e., some being which *does* exist by its own nature. But the world around us can't be this necessary being, since its nonexistence is conceivable. Therefore, the necessary being must transcend the world. And this transcendent being is God.

The first of Cleanthes' four objections (the only one to be discussed here) is that the words "necessary existence" have no meaning.

Cleanthes explains that if, in speaking of a contingent (nonnecessary) being, Demea means a being whose nonexistence is conceivable (in the sense that denying its existence is not a contradiction), then *everything* that exists is a contingent being. For, given any existential statement (e.g., "Bison still exist"), it is *never* a contradiction in terms to deny it. Contrast this with a mathematical proposition, e.g., "The whole is greater than the part": If you deny that, you *are* contradicting yourself, since "greater than its part" is implied by the definition of the term "whole" (i.e., it's a defining property of "whole"). But although mathematical propositions may be necessarily true, they never assert the real existence of anything.

Why can't existence be a defining property of a thing? A Kantian, and Humean, answer would go roughly as follows: To say that something exists is not to characterize it or to add anything to its definition. A definition must answer the question "What is it?" But if you ask me *what* I have in a certain sealed box, and I respond, "Something that exists," I haven't even begun to answer your question (as I would have had I said, say, "something mineral"). To say "X exists" is to say that something in the world *corresponds* to the concept *X;* it does not contribute to the definition of the concept.[21]

So now we can see why the cosmological argument, propounded by Demea, has the same flaw as Descartes' ontological argument: Both employ the same nonsensical "concept," that of a being having *existence* as one of its defining properties. Both misuse the concept of logical necessity, applying it to a question of matter-of-fact and real existence, rather than keeping it in its proper sphere—relations of ideas.

Parts X and XI (The Problem of Evil)

The many twists and turns in these Parts are well worth study and discussion. But in these notes I just want to underline what I take to be their major import, as stated by Philo.

According to Philo, a natural theology based on experience can never yield the conclusion that the Deity has a goodness resembling human goodness. He says that experience suggests, if anything, the very opposite conclusion:

> Look around this universe.... The whole presents nothing but the idea of a blind Nature, impregnated by a great vivifying principle, and pouring forth from her lap, without discernment or parental care, her maimed and abortive children! (p. 74)

But he remains skeptical about *any* theory in this area:

> Let us allow that if the goodness of the Deity (I mean a goodness like the human) could be established on any tolerable reasons *a priori*, these phenomena [see previous quotation], however untoward, would not be sufficient to subvert that principle, but might easily, in some unknown manner, be reconcilable to it. But let us still assert that, as this goodness is not antecedently established, but must be inferred from the phenomena, there can be no grounds for such an inference while there are so many ills in the universe, and while these ills might so easily have been remedied, as far as human understanding can be allowed to judge on such a subject. (p. 74)

In other words, although our experience seems to suggest that the cause of the natural order is an amoral force, blind to human value, our experience is really a poor guide in such matters. For human experience takes in only small slices of reality. In reality, for all we know, the natural world *may* be (in some way incomprehensible to us) the product of a loving God. Faced with these competing hypotheses, the most reasonable response would be skepticism.

Part XII

Near the beginning of this, the last, Part of the *Dialogues,* Philo comes out with the following rather surprising exclamation:

> ... [N]o one ... pays more profound adoration to the Divine Being, as he discovers [reveals] himself to reason in the inexplicable contrivance and artifice of nature. A purpose, an intention, a design strikes everywhere the most careless, the most stupid thinker and no man can be so hardened in absurd systems as at all times to reject it. (p. 77)

It seems that what Philo had been objecting to earlier in the *Dialogues* was not (after all) the argument from design as such, but the uncritical use Cleanthes had made of it. His objections were directed against Cleanthes' use of experimental reasoning to infer, merely from the order in the world, to an anthropomorphic and comprehensible Deity—a Deity with a nature resembling man's moral, as well as intellectual, attributes.[22] His point was that there is absolutely no basis in human experience for such an inference.

Philo, and probably Hume himself, held to a position which has been called *minimal theism,*[23] a position differing "only verbally" from a modest, philosophical atheism:

> That the works of nature bear a great analogy to the productions of art is evident. . . . But as there are also considerable differences, we have reason to suppose a proportional difference in the causes, . . . and if we make it a question whether, on account of these analogies, we can properly call him a *mind* or *intelligence,* notwithstanding the vast difference which may reasonably be supposed between him and human minds, what is this but a mere verbal controversy? (pp. 79–80)

The philosophical theist admits the difference but stresses the similarity, while the philosophical atheist admits the similarity but stresses the difference. Their disagreement is not substantive.

Philo maintains that the whole of natural theology resolves itself into one simple proposition, "That the cause or causes of order in the universe probably bear some remote analogy to human intelligence," and that this proposition "affords no inference that affects human life" (p. 88)—that is, no conclusion follows from it about human destiny or about how people ought to behave morally or politically.

Hume, in other places, argued that ordinary morality is based on natural human sentiments and passions (such as sympathy), not on conjectures of theology or popular religion. And he rejected, as unhealthy and subversive of sound morals, the "supernatural morality" which is based on such conjectures and which is preached in many popular religions. Consider, for example, the following attack on the "monkish [monastic] virtues" in his *Enquiry Concerning the Principles of Morals:*

> And as every quality which is useful or agreeable to ourselves or others is, in common life, allowed to be a part of personal merit, so no other will ever be received where men judge of things by their natural, unprejudiced reason, without the delusive glosses of superstition and false religion. Celibacy, fasting, penance, mortification, self-denial, humility, silence, solitude, and the whole train of monkish virtues—for what reason are they everywhere rejected by men of sense but because they serve to no manner of purpose; neither advance a man's fortune in the world, nor render him a more valuable member of society; neither qualify him for the entertainment of company, nor increase his power of self-enjoyment? We observe, on the contrary, that they cross all these desirable ends, stupefy the understanding and harden the heart, obscure the fancy and sour the temper. We justly, therefore, transfer them to the opposite column and place them in the catalogue of vices; nor has any superstition force sufficient among men of the world to pervert entirely these natural sentiments. A gloomy, harebrained enthusiast [fanatic], after his death, may have a place in the calendar [of saints] but will scarcely ever be admitted when alive into intimacy and society, except by those who are as delirious and dismal as himself. (Sec. IX, Part I)

The *philosophical religion* of Philo (and Hume) involves a feeling of awe in the face of the order of nature, and an attitude of reverence for its mysterious Source. Philo contrasts this attitude with the "arrogant and presumptuous" mentality of those religious dogmatists who claim to have arrived at a clear and distinct knowledge of God's nature and purposes. Such a claim is contrary to the Academic skepticism that he had advocated in Part I, and to the "sound piety" that he commends in this Part.

Philo, at the end of the *Dialogues,* stresses the very limited knowledge of God available to natural human intelligence, and expresses the pious hope that "heaven would be pleased to . . . alleviate this profound ignorance by affording some more particular revelation to mankind" (p. 89).[24] Many people at Philo's time, and today, believe that heaven *has in fact* provided such a revelation through the Christian religion. This religion is supposed to provide mankind with a rather determinate knowledge of God and of the future state (heaven or hell) which God has in store for mankind. But is this, or any other claim to supernatural revelation, credible?

Many Christians would argue that Christianity is credible because of the evidence provided by the signs and wonders of its founders. But, in his essay on miracles, Hume scrutinized that evidence and found it wanting. He agreed that no reasonable person could believe the Christian religion without miracles, but he argued that no one could reasonably believe the miracle stories in the first place. He concluded, ironically, that whoever is moved by *faith* to assent to the Christian religion

> ... is conscious of a continued miracle in his own person, which subverts all the principles of his understanding, and gives him a determination to believe what is most contrary to custom and experience. (*EHU*, p. 90)

Hume's view seems to have been this: People with a healthy respect for the principles of human understanding will shy away from this supernatural faith, and be content with a religion that is *not* contrary to custom and experience— with a modest and natural religion.

AN OVERVIEW OF HUME'S PHILOSOPHY

From the premises (1) that sense perception is the only basis for factual knowledge, (2) that all claims to factual knowledge beyond the immediate deliverances of perception are based on the relation of cause and effect, and (3) that perception is powerless to reveal causal (i.e., necessary) connections between the objects given in perception, Hume arrived at the conclusion that there can be no justification—no rational basis—for claims to factual knowledge about anything beyond the immediate impressions of perception.

This conclusion, if accepted, would undermine belief in both the existence of an objective material reality corresponding to our perceptual ideas, and the validity of all inferences from past experience to future probabilities—beliefs which are fundamental to the everyday and scientific operations of the human mind. But, Hume continues, this skeptical conclusion will never be accepted *in practice* by men of sense, no matter how well founded it is *in theory*. For the beliefs which it would subvert are so deeply rooted in everyday human life and practice that no mere process of reasoning could possibly dislodge them. ("Nature is always too strong for principle," *EHU*, Sec. IX.)

To the extent that they lead to conclusions about matters remote from the natural world of everyday life and practice, the arguments of metaphysical philosophers are not safe from the corrosive power of skeptical counterarguments. Such metaphysical arguments would include Cleanthes' inference from the natural world to a transcendent and providential Designer, as well as Leibniz's more ambitious arguments to the reality of monads, the perfection of the world, and the assembly of all spirits (the City of God).[25] But they would *not* include Philo's "minimal theism," his inference from the order in the world to an immanent principle of order "which probably bears some remote analogy to human intelligence" (p. 88). For this inference is so modest and irresistible "that all objections [to it] appear mere cavils and sophisms" (p. 66).

Devotees of popular religions claim a knowledge of God and his purposes which goes far beyond the modest, rationally irresistible inference warranted by a just natural theology. They claim that their beliefs come from on high, from a special, supernatural revelation. But in doing so they are reduced to dogmatic assertion. For they have abandoned the ground of natural human experience and practice, and therefore the common ground on which all efforts at justification must rest.

FOR FURTHER READING

A. G. N. FLEW, "Hume," in D. J. O'Connor, ed., *A Critical History of Western Philosophy*. Glencoe, Ill.: The Free Press, 1964.

G. A. C. GASKIN, *Hume's Philosophy of Religion*. New York: Barnes & Noble, 1978. This, along with Flew's article, has been most helpful to me in my own study of Hume.

NORMAN KEMP SMITH, *The Philosophy of David Hume*. London: Macmillan, 1941. A classic, if somewhat advanced, study.

H. H. PRICE, *Hume's Theory of the External World*. Oxford: Oxford University Press, 1940. Another classic interpretation.

WILLIAM J. ABRAHAM, *An Introduction to the Philosophy of Religion*. Englewood Cliffs, N.J.: Prentice-Hall, 1985. Chapter 13 contains a short critique of Hume on miracles. See the listing under Hume, in the index, for further relevant material.

DIOGENES ALLEN, "Natural Evil and the Love of God," in *Religious Studies*, Vol. 16 (1980), pp. 439–456. Presents a perspective on the problem of evil profoundly different from Hume's.

QUESTIONS

1. Write a one-page summary of Section I of the *Enquiry* ("Of the Different Species of Philosophy").

2. *Define:* perceptions, impressions, ideas; the principles of connection among ideas.

3. The "missing shade of blue" discussed by Hume in *Enquiry,* Section II seems to present a counterexample to the empiricist thesis that every idea is a copy of an antecedent impression. How does Hume deal with this? Do you find his response satisfactory?

4. Using several examples of each, distinguish *relations of ideas* from *matters of fact and real existence.*

5. What, according to Hume, is the nature of the evidence which assures us of any real existence or matter of fact, beyond the present testimony of our senses, or the records of our memory? (Go into some detail.)

6. Sum up Hume's account of the idea of necessary connection.

7. What is the dilemma of freedom and determinism, and how does Hume resolve it? Are you satisfied with Hume's resolution? According to Aristotle, "we do not praise or blame for what is due to necessity, or chance, or nature, but only for what we ourselves are causes of" (*Eudemian Ethics*, 1223a). How would Hume respond?

8. Summarize and evaluate "Of Miracles." Do you think Hume's argument poses any threat to religious faith?

9. What was Hume's position on the topic of skepticism regarding the senses? Compare with Descartes, Locke, and Berkeley.

10. Summarize Cleanthes' argument from design and some of Philo's objections to it. What do you think of the argument?

11. State Demea's *a priori* argument and two of Cleanthes' objections to it.

12. What is the "problem of evil"? What implications does it have for belief in God, according to Philo? Do you agree with Philo?

13. What was Philo's conception of *true religion?* What do you think of it?

14. Write a two- or three-page paper on Hume's short essay "Of the Immortality of the Soul" (pp. 91–97 in the Hackett ed.). Summarize the arguments, relate them (where possible) to the conclusion of the *Enquiry* and *Dialogues,* and evaluate them.

15. Write a two- or three-page paper on Hume's short essay "Of Suicide" (pp. 97–105). Summarize the arguments, relate them (where possible) to the conclusion of the *Enquiry* and *Dialogues,* and evaluate them.

16. Early in his classic of Christian apologetics, *Orthodoxy* (1908), G. K. Chesterton tries to convey the content of his own natural religion and the circumstances that had led him to adopt it. There are interesting and instructing affinities, as well as great differences, between Chesterton and Hume on the topic of religion. Write a paper bringing out and discussing some of these affinities and differences. Suggestions: (a) Compare what Chesterton says in Chapter IV ("The Ethics of Elfland") with Sections IV and VII of the *Enquiry* and with Part XII of the *Dialogues;* (b) compare Chesterton Chapter V ("The Flag of the World") with Hume's essay on suicide.

NOTES

[1]All references to the *Enquiry Concerning Human Understanding (EHU)* are to pages in the Hackett edition, edited by Eric Steinberg (Indianapolis: Hackett, 1977). I have modernized some of the spelling and punctuation in my quotations.

[2]From the last page of Hume's *An Abstract of A Treatise of Human Nature* (1740). In Charles W. Hendel, ed. *An Inquiry Concerning Human Understanding* (Indianapolis: Bobbs-Merrill, 1955), p. 198.

[3]Kantian = from Immanuel Kant, whose philosophy is the subject of Chapter 7. Note that Kant's term "analytic truth" is synonymous with Leibniz's "truths of reason," as well as with Hume's "relations of ideas."

[4]Cf. Ludwig Wittgenstein, *On Certainty.* (New York: Harper & Row, 1969), Sec. 130.

[5]On the problem of sorting out and reconciling the various things Hume says on the topic of the reasonableness of inductive inferences, see M. J. Ferreira's "Hume's Naturalism—'Proof' and Practice," in *Philosophical Quarterly,* 35 (1985), pp. 45–57.

[6]The *Ethics* of Spizona, Part V, is a notable instance of a philosophical attempt to control or alter these sentiments.

[7]Two valuable, but somewhat opposed, interpretations of Hume on liberty and necessity are: Paul Russell, "On the Naturalism of Hume's Reconciling Project'" (*Mind,* 1983, pp. 593–600) and Antony Flew, *Hume's Philosophy of Belief* (London: Routledge & Kegan Paul, 1961), Chap. 7. I am indebted to both works, especially the former.

[8]See Chapter 2, p. 29.

[9]*On Certainty* (New York: Harper & Row, 1972), Sec. 287 and 359.

[10]*Philosophical Investigations* (New York: Macmillan, 1953), Sec. 473.

[11]I am indebted here to a fine article by Oswald Hanfling, "Hume and Wittgenstein," in *Impressions of Empiricism,* edited by Godfrey Vesey (New York: St. Martin's Press, 1976).

[12]From *Philosophy* (April 1974, Vol. 49, no. 188), Renford Bambrough, editor. Reprinted with permission of Cambridge University Press. Copyright 1974, The Royal Institute of Philosophy.

[13]This is a form of the relativity argument, which was touched on in the Introduction to this book.

[14]See pp. 112–113 (Hackett ed.) for Hume's defense of this restriction. If Hume is right, then Locke was wrong when he stressed the possibility of demonstrative knowledge about the ethical subjects of right and wrong.

[15]This will be discussed later, on pp. 110–112.

[16]Page references are to Richard H. Popkin's edition of the *Dialogues* (Indianapolis: Hackett, 1980). I have modernized the spelling and punctuation in my quotations.

[17]Demea's reaction to anthropomorphism is similar to that of the first philosopher of religion, Xenophanes, in the sixth century B.C.: "If oxen or lions had hands which enabled them to draw and paint pictures as men do, they would portray their gods as having bodies like their own. . . . [But] God is really one, supreme among gods and men, not at all like mortals in body or in mind " (Wheelwright translation).

[18]See Locke's *Essay:* II, xxiii, 2 (p. 64 above).

[19]Spinoza ascribed the first three of these traditional attributes to God (and Nature) on the basis of *a priori* rather than empirical reasoning. This rationalist aspect of Spinoza's thought is, of course, directly at variance with Hume's basic epistemology.

[20]See Chapter 1, p. 15, above.

[21]This formulation owes something to the fine paper by Terence Penelhum, "Divine Necessity," in Donald R. Burrill, ed., *The Cosmological Arguments* (Garden City, N.Y.: Doubleday, 1967).

[22]Compare with Spinoza's analysis of popular anthropomorphic theology in *Ethics* I, Appendix (reprinted above).

[23]See J. C. A. Gaskin, *Hume's Philosophy of Religion* (New York: Barnes & Noble, 1978). My exposition of the *Dialogues,* and of this Part in particular, is heavily indebted to Gaskin's excellent study.

[24]Compare with the following from Hume's essay, "The Skeptic" (1742): ". . . An abstract, invisible object, like that which *natural* religion alone presents to us cannot long actuate the mind, or be of any moment in life. To render the passion of continuance, we must find some method of affecting the senses and imagination, and must embrace some *historical,* as well as *philosophical* account of the divinity. Popular superstitions and observances are ever found to be of use in this particular."

[25]Hume scrutinizes the Leibnizian "best of all possible worlds" theory in *EHU,* Part II of Sec. VIII, especially pp. 67–68.

chapter 7

KANT

THE CRITICAL PHILOSOPHY

With Immanuel Kant (1724–1804) we come to the end of the classical period of modern philosophy. His "critical philosophy" presented an attractive alternative to both British empiricism and Continental rationalism.

Born into a poor family of the Pietist (a reformed Lutheran) faith, Kant spent his enitre life in his native city of Königsberg, Prussia (now Kaliningrad, Russia). Unlike the earlier moderns, he made his living by teaching philosophy. And it was during his tenure as a professor in the University of Königsberg that he wrote the following volumes, which were to make him world-famous and rank him among the very greatest philosophers of all times:

> *Critique of Pure Reason* (first ed. 1781, second ed. 1787), a monumental treatise on epistemology and metaphysics.
>
> *Prolegomena to Any Future Metaphysics that Will be Able to Come Forward as Science* (1783), a much shorter and somewhat different version of Kant's epistemology and metaphysics. "Prolegomena" means "critical preliminaries to the study of a subject."
>
> *Foundations of the Metaphysics of Morals* (1785), an investigation of the basic *a priori* principles of moral judgment.

Critique of Practical Reason (1788), a more elaborate treatment of moral philosophy.

Critique of Judgment (1790), an analysis of our aesthetic and teleological experience of nature and art.

The first *Critique* is an investigation of the nature and limits of "pure," i.e., *a priori*, knowledge. The question is: What can we know about reality prior to empirical investigation? And the answer given is, in short: (1) We can know that reality, insofar as it can be an object of knowledge at all must conform to certain *a priori* conditions laid down by the knowing subject, conditions without which empirical knowledge of even the simplest sort would be impossible. (2) All other claims to substantive *a priori* knowledge, such as are found in rationalistic demonstrations of God and immortality, are based on illusion.

Following the empiricist principle, according to which all concepts arise out of experience, Hume had concluded that no claims to factual knowledge can be rationally justified, except for the simplest judgments of perception and memory. Responding to Hume, Kant argued that if the empiricist principle were really valid, then *all* knowledge, even the simplest perceptual knowledge, would be impossible. From this he concluded that the empiricist principle cannot be valid. And he went on to develop a theory according to which all perceptual knowledge presupposes the validity of certain nonempirical concepts and *a priori* principles. This theory, along with his account of how *a priori* knowledge is possible, will be explained in Part One of this chapter.

Kant's account of the nature of *a priori* knowledge had devastating implications for rationalistic metaphysics. Some of these will be explained in Part Two.

The reading for this chapter is from the beginning of the *Critique of Pure Reason.* In it Kant summarizes his case against rationalistic metaphysics while assuring us that its destruction will pose no threat to ethico-religious faith.

PART ONE: THE NATURE AND FUNCTION
OF *A PRIORI* KNOWLEDGE

Judgment and Knowledge

Here we define some important technical terms of Kantian philosophy, starting with "judgment."

A *judgment* is a truth-claim; truth-claims are statements or propositions, as opposed to questions, suppositions, and imperatives. There are two radically different types of judgment: analytic and synthetic. These differ in the types of truth-claims they make.

An *analytic judgment* is (when true at all) true in virtue of the definitions of its terms. Consider the example: "All sisters are females." Note that its predicate (females) is contained in the definition, or analysis, of its subject (female siblings).

It is a contradiction in terms to deny an analytic truth. For example, to deny that sisters are females is to say that *female* siblings are *not female*.

Synthetic judgments are nonanalytic. Consider the example: "All sisters quarrel." If we deny this, we may be making a false judgment—but we are not contradicting ourselves.

In a synthetic judgment something is ascribed to a subject that wasn't already implicit in its definition. It can therefore add to our knowledge of things. An analytic judgment, on the other hand, simply makes explicit what's already implicit in the concept of its subject. And so it cannot add to our knowledge of things.

Justified truth-claims make up the body of *knowledge*. And as truth-claims can be justified in either of two ways, *a posteriori* or *a priori*, there are two distinct types of knowledge.

A posteriori knowledge is empirical, i.e., justified by way of evidence drawn from sense experience (observation or experiment). Empirical generalizations, such as "All sisters quarrel," are obvious examples of this type of knowledge.

A priori knowledge is nonempirical: It does not require justification by way of observation or experiment. Here mathematical propositions provide a ready store of examples.

While *a posteriori* knowledge is *contingent*—true for the actual world, as revealed in sense experience—*a priori* knowledge is *necessary*—true for all conceivable worlds.

A Priori Knowledge of Synthetic Truths

Kant's analytic/synthetic distinction corresponds to Hume's distinction between relations of ideas and matters of fact. But Hume held (to use Kant's terminology) that the analytic/synthetic distinction is equivalent to the *a priori* / *a posteriori* distinction. He held, in other words, that all *a priori* knowledge is analytic and that all synthetic knowledge is *a posteriori*. Kant denied this, arguing that there is a third legitimate kind of knowledge: *a priori* knowledge of synthetic truths. For example: "Every event is caused." This proposition is not an empirical generalization, like "Smoking causes cancer"; nor is it analytic, like "Every effect is caused."

It is nonsensical to deny that "Every *effect* is caused," because the notion of an uncaused effect is a contradiction in terms. And while it is also nonsensical to deny that every *event* has a cause, it is not so for the same reason. For to speak of an "uncaused event" is not a contradiction in terms. And yet it *is* somehow illogical, or nonsensical, to speak that way—as the

following story from the contemporary Kant scholar, W. H. Walsh, illustrates:

> I am being driven by a friend in a motor-car when, without warning, the en-
> gine stops and the car comes to a standstill. I ask my friend what has hap-
> pened. He replies that the car has stopped for no reason at all. I laugh
> politely.... [1]

Kant argued that there are *categories of the understanding,* certain basic forms
of judgment, which serve as criteria for distinguishing sense from nonsense.
Causality is one such category. *Substance* is another, equally important, one;
its role in our thinking comes out in the following, longer, story from Walsh:

> A calls on B at an awkward moment when B has dropped his collar stud and
> cannot find it. "I had it in my hand a minute ago," he tells his friend, "so it
> can't be far off." The search goes on for some time without success, until A
> suddenly asks B what makes him think the stud is there to be found. Control-
> ling himself, B explains that he had the stud in his hand and was trying to do
> up his collar when it slipped from his fingers; that there are no holes in the
> floor; that the windows of the room are unusually high; and that if the stud
> had come to pieces he must certainly have come across some bit of it after
> looking for so long. "Ah," says A, "but have you considered the possibility
> that it may have vanished without trace?" "Vanished without trace?" asks B:
> "do you mean turned into gaseous form, gone off like a puff of smoke or
> something of that sort? Collar-studs don't do things like that." "No, that isn't
> what I mean," A assures him gravely; "I mean literally vanished without trace,
> passed clean out of existence." Words fail B at this point, but it is clear from
> the look he gives his friend that he takes him either to be making an ill-timed
> joke or to be talking downright nonsense....

The principle of causality ("Every event has a cause") and the principle of substance ("Nothing vanishes without a trace"), illustrated in the preceding stories, were for Kant prime examples of synthetic knowledge *a priori.* As true synthetic judgments, they convey information about the world
that we experience; as *a priori* judgments, they are not based on experience
of the world.

Kant's Copernican Revolution

The pivotal question of the *Critique of Pure Reason* is: How can there
possibly be any knowledge of the world which is not based on the perception, or experimental investigation, of it? In other words, how can any claim
to synthetic knowledge *a priori* be justified?

Kant says that the solution to this problem requires a revolutionary
change of perspective, a change in philosophy analogous to the Copernican
revolution in astronomy:

> Hitherto it has been assumed that all our knowledge must conform to objects.
> But all attempts to extend our knowledge of objects by establishing something

in regard to them *a priori*, by means of concepts, have, on this assumption, ended in failure. We must therefore make trial whether we may not have more success in the tasks of metaphysics,[2] if we suppose that objects must conform to our knowledge. This would agree better with what is desired, namely that it should be possible to have knowledge of objects *a priori*, determining something in regard to them prior to their being given. We should then be proceeding precisely on the lines of Copernicus' primary hypothesis. Failing of satisfactory progress in explaining the movements of the heavenly bodies on the supposition that they all revolved round the spectator, he tried whether he might not have better success if he made the spectator to revolve and the stars to remain at rest. (B xvi)[3]

Knowing that every object in the world must conform to the principles of causality and substance would be impossible if knowledge must always conform itself to objects—that is, if all knowledge of the world must await empirical verification. But—and this is Kant's Copernican revolution—it *is* possible precisely to the extent that objects of knowledge must always conform to certain conditions *set by the knowing subject.* These conditions, expressed in categorical[4] principles, apply to the world of experience, because without them there would *be* no world of experience to know.

Knowledge of the world comes in two essentially different, but related, forms, according to Kant: The first, called *empirical* knowledge, is expressed in synthetic judgments *a posteriori.* Such judgments must conform to observable fact in order to be true. The second, called *transcendental* knowledge, provides the framework within which empirical objects are experienced and *a posteriori* judgments justified. It is expressed in synthetic judgments *a priori*, such as the principle of causality. All objects of knowledge must conform to such principles in order to *count* as objects of knowledge. For example: We do not count a dream experience of flying cats as an object of knowledge, or allow it to count against the empirical generalization that no cats fly—we dismiss "dream cats" as subjective phantasms. Why? Because they may vanish without a trace, thus violating the principle of substance. And they may pop into existence without any necessary determining condition, thus violating the principle of causality.[5]

In its empirical function, the mind derives laws from nature; in its transcendental function, it prescribes laws to nature:

> ... [W]e must not seek the universal laws of nature in nature by means of experience, but conversely must seek nature, as to its universal conformity to law, in the conditions of the possibility of experience....
> ... *[T]he understanding does not derive its laws (a priori) from, but prescribes them to, nature.*[6]

It must be stressed that these laws have no *absolute* validity. Their jurisdiction extends only to *the phenomenal order.* And the phenomenal order is something *constructed* by the human mind through the application of the *a priori* laws of the understanding to *appearances,* i.e., to the material given by the senses. Thus we know that these laws apply *to phenomena.* But as to "how things may be in themselves, apart from the representations through which they affect us, [that] is entirely outside our sphere of knowledge" (A 190/B 235). And it would be absurd if we "conceded no things in themselves or declared our experience to be the only possible mode of knowing things ... [or took] the principles of the possibility of experience for universal conditions of things in themselves" (*Prolegomena* 351).

The *A Priori* Forms of Sensibility

We can know about things only so far as we are affected by them. The mind's faculty of being affected by things is called *intuition*. The forms of human intuition are space and time. Therefore we can gain no knowledge of things transcending space and time.

The intuition of *time* is presupposed to all experience whatsoever, *inner* (introspective) or *outer* (sense experience).

The intuition of *space* is presupposed to all experience of external objects, because that by which we judge objects to be external ("outer") is their position in space.

To say that everything external (objective) is located in space is to make a synthetic *a priori* statement. And, like all other such statements, it is justifiable only as a claim about the way (form) in which things appear to us. Thus we have no right to claim that spatiality is a necessary feature of things as they are in themselves (independent of our way of perceiving them). And so we must acknowledge the abstract possibility of beings with a different form of intuition from our own—beings with a nonspatial (or atemporal) way of perceiving things. But we must also acknowledge that it is only within a spatio-temporal framework that *we* have experience and knowledge of things. For we can give no *content* to the notion of a real thing which is yet nowhere, nor to the notion of an experience which involves no temporal succession. When the rationalists talked of "timeless, unextended substances" (recall the *monads* of Leibniz), they were transgressing the bounds of sense—passing off empty formal concepts for genuine concepts of objects.[7]

The human mind's spatio-temporally structured intuitive faculty is called *sensibility*. Its categorially structured thinking or judging faculty is called *understanding*. Knowledge is the offspring of sensibility and understanding:

> Without sensibility no object would be given to us, without understanding no object would be thought. Thoughts without content are empty, intuitions without concepts are blind. It is, therefore, just as necessary to make our concepts sensible, that is, to add the object to them in intuition, as to make our intuitions intelligible, that is, to bring them under concepts. These two powers or capacities cannot exchange their functions. The understanding can intuit nothing, the senses can think nothing. Only through their union can knowledge arise. (A 51/B 75)

The Deduction of the Categories

Kant gives an (allegedly) complete list of all categories (or "pure concepts") of the understanding in the following Table of Categories (B 106):

I

Of Quantity
Unity
Plurality
Totality

II

Of Quality
Reality
Negation
Limitation

III

Of Relation
Of Inherence and Subsistence
(substance and accident)
Of Causality and Dependence
(cause and effect)
Of Community (reciprocity between
agent and patient)

IV

Of Modality
Possibility—Impossibility
Existence—Nonexistence
Necessity—Contingency

Kant claims to have derived this table from "the logical forms of judgment."[8] But we will not discuss that. We will discuss the much more important question of the justification of the categories, focusing mainly on Kant's justification of substance and causality.

To justify categories is to prove that they necessarily apply to the phenomenal world, i.e., to everything that could be an object of perception for us. Such a proof would have to show that there could *be* no objects of perception unless the categories applied to them. It would have to show that without the categories our subjective perceptual data would have no objective meaning, i.e., could not refer to *objects* of perception at all.[9]

We begin our elucidation of this proof—of this *transcendental deduction,* as Kant called it—by asking *how* the application of the categories of substance and causality allows us to assign objective meaning to our perceptual data.

Kant approaches the question by reminding us that the objects of perception are constantly changing over the course of time; he then argues that we could not coherently describe this change, or even our subjective impression of it, without presupposing material substance and causality. He argues, in other words, that Berkeleyan immaterialism can give no coherent account of change.

When we see something change, we observe a succession of contrary sensible states and ascribe them to one and the same object. Thus, in seeing that a piece of wax is being melted we are judging that something opaque and solid is becoming liquid and transparent, and are presupposing that something—some stuff or matter—is persisting throughout the change.[10]

"Material substance" means "the stuff which persists throughout all changes." In speaking of the substance of things, we are referring to the basic material reality of all natural (i.e., changing) things, i.e., to something which underlies change and makes it possible.

A material object (such as a piece of wax) has both immediately perceivable, sensible, features (a particular shape, color, etc.) and inferred, dispositional features (capacity to change color, shape, etc.). The latter features are ascribed to its underlying nature and might be called its *material* properties; the former features belong to its immediately perceivable nature and are called its *sensible properties*.[11]

The material properties of objects provide the underlying grounds for the regular successions of sensible properties that we observe in the natural world. For example, it is the flexibility of a stick which enables it to be at first straight and then bent.

The matter and the material properties of an object are not sensible features of the object. And so we can have no ideas of them, in Berkeley's sense of idea. For they are known only by way of *a priori* concepts, i.e., categories of the understanding.[12]

Like every good empiricist, Berkeley tried to follow the maxim of epistemological caution known as Ockham's Razor, a maxim which forbids the unnecessary postulation of nonempirical factors.[13] Kant agreed with the maxim, but disagreed that it applies to material substance and material properties. For, as we have seen, he argued that it is *necessary* to posit them in order to account for even the simplest judgments of perception. Let us develop this argument further, using the judgment, "The solid wax has vaporized," as our example.

In that judgment we are saying that something which was potentially gaseous is now actually gaseous. We have sensed a succession of qualities (from solidity to liquidity to gaseousness) and predicated each quality of one and the same "something." And, although this "something" was not at first actually gaseous, we must have judged that it was *potentially* so. And so we have appealed to three nonsensible factors: the "something" (substance) and the potentiality (possibility, or passive power) and the actuality (existence). Each of these factors has a place in Kant's Table of Categories.[14]

In saying of a stick that it has been bent, we are not saying that one stick, a straight one, has been *replaced* by another stick, a bent one. We are saying of one and the same "flexible something" that it was straight and is now bent. Thus we distinguish *real change* from the mere *substitution* of one sensible thing for another. And in doing so, we are employing *a priori* concepts, including (to introduce a new one) the category of *negation*. Let me now explain this.

To perceive that a stick is being bent, we must be able to represent the fact that at one time it was straight and at a later time it was *not*, i.e., we must be able to *see the stick as* something that used to be straight but is *no longer* straight. Thus, in order to perceive the event of a stick being bent—or indeed any event—we must be able to represent an alteration from one state to another (straight→bent), and in order to do *that,* we must be able to represent negation (absence). But, since we can have no sensory representation (mental picture) of negation, we must have a nonsensory representation of it (an *a priori* concept). Thus, to know that *b* begins to be, and *a* ceases to be, is to know something not wholly present to the senses or represented in sensuous imagination.

A famous example from Kant himself which illustrates the role of the concept of negation in the perception of motion is that of observing a ship moving downstream. In seeing it now, at point *b*, we see it as no longer at the point, *a*, where it was a moment earlier. At the present moment, we have a sense impression of the ship at point *b*, but we have no sense impression of its no longer being at point *a*, nor of its not having been at *b* a moment earlier.

I described that example mainly in order to contrast it with another famous example from Kant, namely that of someone looking over a house. This will help us to understand how the principle of causality enables us to identify objective happenings, i.e., events.

Contrast standing on a riverbank, watching a ship move downstream, with standing in front of a house, looking first at the roof, then at the second floor windows, etc. In both cases there is a succession in our sensory awareness—a "succession of perceptions," as Kant called it. But only the first succession is judged to have objective significance, i.e., to represent a corresponding change in the object of perception. And it is judged to have this significance only because it (in contrast with the second succession) is regarded as *irreversible,* and therefore *subject to a rule,* and therefore *determined by causes*—or so Kant argues in the "Second Analogy," one of the more intriguing and controversial sections of the *Critique.* Here is the passage:

> . . . I see a ship move down stream. My perception of its lower position follows upon the perception of its position higher up in the stream, and it is impossible that in the apprehension of this appearance the ship should first be perceived lower down in the stream and afterwards higher up. The order in which the perceptions succeed one another in apprehension is in this instance determined, and to this order apprehension is bound down. In the

previous example of a house my perceptions could begin with the apprehension of the roof and end with the basement, or could begin from below and end above. . . . In the series of these perceptions there was thus no determinate order specifying at what point I must begin in order to connect the manifold [multiplicity] empirically. But in the perception of an event there is always a rule which makes the order in which the perceptions (in the apprehension of this appearance) follow upon one another a *necessary* order. (A 192–193/B 237–238)

Kant is arguing that, in order to perceive an event *as such*, we must make use of the principle according to which whatever we judge to be an *event* (an objective happening) we must also judge to be *caused*, i.e., preceded in time by "something upon which it follows according to a rule" (A 190). In developing this argument, Kant proceeds indirectly, asking us to

. . . suppose that there is nothing antecedent to an event, upon which it must follow according to a rule. All succession of perception would then be only in the apprehension, that is would be merely subjective, and would never enable us to determine objectively which perceptions are those that really precede and which are those that follow. We should then have only a play of representations, relating to no object. . . . I could not then assert that two states follow upon one another in the field of appearance, but only that one apprehension follows upon the other. . . .

If, then, we experience that something happens, we in so doing always presuppose that something precedes it, on which it follows according to a rule. Otherwise I should not say of the object that it follows. For mere succession in my apprehension, if there be no rule determining the succession in relation to something that precedes, does not justify me in assuming any succession in the object. I render my subjective synthesis of apprehension objective only by reference to a rule in accordance with which the appearances in their succession, that is, as they happen, are determined by the preceding state. The experience of an event (i.e., of anything as *happening*) is itself possible only on this assumption. (A 194–195/B 239–240)

Hume thought that the principle of causality was a generalization from our experience of events.[15] But if Kant's argument is sound, then all perception of events, and consequently all generalization from experience, *presupposes* the principle of causality. Kant's answer to Hume is (to put it in other words) that the principle of causality is *presupposed by* the perception of events, not *derived from* it.

Let us review Kant's reasoning by setting it out as an argument in five steps:

1.   The perception of an event requires *successive perceptions* of an object.
2.   It also requires the perception of *successive states of the object,* and (since all apprehension is successive) this can never be determined on the basis of the successiveness of the perceptions themselves.

(The apprehension of the house, as well as the apprehension of the moving ship, involves a succession of perceptions. And yet we think of ourselves as perceiving successive states of an object only in the latter case.)

3. In order to consider a succession of perceptions as perception of successive states of an object, it is necessary to regard their order as *irreversible.*

     (If I judge that I'm perceiving the event of a change in position of a ship from point A at time t_1 to point B at t_2, then I must also think of the order of my perceptions as determined—I must think of it as AB and *not* BA. If I reverse the order in imagination, then I'm thinking of a different event—that of the ship sailing upstream, rather than downstream.)

4. To regard perceptions as irreversible in this way is to subject them to an *a priori* rule—the rule that, given *A*, *B* will invariably follow. This is the causal rule.

5. Since it is only by subjecting our perceptions to this rule that we can regard them as containing the representation of an event, it follows that the event itself (as the object represented) is likewise subjected to the rule. Thus the rule, the principle of causality, has objective validity.[16]

Illusion and Reality

Like Descartes before them, the British empiricists were motivated by the desire to avoid falsehood and precipitous judgment. But, unlike Descartes, they attempted to derive all knowledge of the world from *sensorily evident* "impressions," believing that these alone provide certain and indubitable knowledge of things. Now with Berkeley and Hume, it became clear that to talk about causal connections between changing states, or about a substance in which sensible quantities inhere, is to talk about what is not sensorily evident. And so empiricists, from Berkeley on, tried to do without those factors in their accounts of the world.

We have seen that Kant differed from the empiricists in claiming that it is *necessary* to posit those, and other nonempirical factors, if we are to account for even the simplest judgments of experience—judgments such as "The ship has moved downstream," or "The stick is now bent." But we have yet to see how he might reply to a Truly Determined Empiricist, i.e., to someone who objected to his arguments along the following lines:

So much the worse for your "judgments of experience"! *If* I chose to make such judgments, *then* I would be making claims to the effect that what *seems* to me true of an object really *is* true of an object (e.g., that the stick which *looks* bent really *is* bent). And I can agree with you that making such claims would indeed commit me to the validity of your "*a priori* categories." But I do not make such claims! I do not venture *any* claim to objective knowledge, because I want to remain on the firm ground of my own indubitable and incorrigible immediate impressions!

These are the words of one who really believes in the possibility of the "evil genius," and yet really doubts the validity of the *a priori* concepts by means of which Descartes had claimed to demonstrate that no such malign deity actually exists.

Kant, like Descartes himself after the Third Meditation, rejected the evil genius hypothesis. But his grounds for rejecting it were totally different from Descartes'.

Descartes' evil genius hypothesis embodies a conception of truth according to which it is possible that we are always believing false propositions, even when we have the best possible evidence for their truth. For it is imagined that what, from a human point of view, constitutes the best possible evidence for the truth of a belief, may count for nothing from the superior point of view of a Deceiver God.

It was under the influence of his famous hypothesis that Descartes felt it necessary to prove the existence of a God who hates deception and who therefore makes truth accessible to his creatures. In other words, it was his peculiar conception of truth which inspired his search for an extraordinary metaphysical foundation for ordinary empirical beliefs.

Kant's reply is that no attempt to demonstrate the falsity of the evil genius hypothesis could possibly succeed, because the hypothesis in question is neither false *nor* true, but simply *meaningless*.

The evil genius hypothesis prompts us to suppose that possibly *none* of our experiences have the objective reference which they seem to have, and that consequently all of our experiences are purely subjective and essentially illusory. But to suppose that *all* of our experiences are purely subjective and essentially illusory would be to empty the words "subjective" and "illusory" of their meaning. For it would take away their use to *contrast* one thing with another. It would be like supposing that *all* "diamonds" have always been *fake* diamonds, or that all "low notes" have always been *high* notes.

The distinction between veridical (objective, true) perception and illusory (merely subjective, false) perception is applicable *in particular cases:* for example, in the case of distinguishing "seeing a bent stick" from "having an optical illusion of a bent stick," or of "seeing an oasis" from " 'seeing' a mirage." But the distinction collapses if applied universally to *all perceptions*. For it is only as contrasted with veridical perception (the normal) that we can talk about illusory perception (the abnormal). And so we do not understand the hypothesis that maybe all oases have always been mirages any more than we understand the suggestion that maybe all currency has always been counterfeit.

It makes no sense to suggest that an experience could obey all of our rules for being veridical—conformity with laws of causality and conservation, etc. (i.e., conformity with the categories of the understanding)—and yet *in fact* be illusory.[17] To make such a suggestion is to attempt to apply a conceptual distinction outside the sphere of possible experience, i.e., outside the sphere where it has its meaning.

Let us return to our Truly Determined Empiricist. We can now perceive the emptiness of his skeptical attitude concerning all objective judgments and of his cautious determination to restrict himself to purely subjective judgments. Both the skeptical attitude and the cautious determination were based on the supposition that *all* objective judgments may be illusory—a supposition which subverts the contrast between *objective* and *subjective*, evacuating the meaning from *both* terms. The Truly Determined Empiricist is therefore in no position to be making even subjective judgments!

If I can speak *only* of what I think—of the impressions in my own conscious mind, how things seem, etc.—then I can speak of nothing at all—not even of those subjective impressions. And so our Truly Determined Empiricist must resign himself to silence.

If I cannot be sure that the *external*, objective world exists, then I cannot be sure that the *internal*, subjective world of my own mind exists. From this we can see that Descartes, through his *cogito* argument, has arrived at the same dead end as did our Truly Determined Empiricist. And so he should join with the latter in a total renunciation of speech and thought.[18]

PART TWO: THE LIMITS OF *A PRIORI* KNOWLEDGE

Result of the Deduction of the Categories

The categories of the understanding are rules for the synthesis (unification) of the spatio-temporally ordered multiplicity of sensuous intuitions. And the product of this synthesis is *experience,* as Kant explains in the following passage:

> We cannot *think* an object without categories; we cannot *know* an object so thought without perceptions that correspond to categories. Now, all our perceptions are sensuous, and therefore all our knowledge of objects that are presented in perception is empirical. But empirical knowledge is experience. *Hence there can be no a priori knowledge, except of objects that are capable of entering into experience.* (B 165–166)[19]

The emphasized sentence states what Kant entitles the "Result of the Deduction of the Categories." It is a result which, if valid, has the following far-reaching implication for *metaphysics,* the would-be science of the *a priori* structure of the world: Metaphysics is possible as a science only if it limits itself to giving an account of the *a priori* structure of the *empirical* (phenomenal) world.

In other words, since the competence of pure (*a priori*) reason extends only to what is universally and necessarily presupposed in experience, only a *transcendental* metaphysics—only a Kantian-type metaphysics of experience—is possible as a science. Therefore *transcendent* metaphysics—a metaphysics of supersensible, timeless realities, in the rationalist style—is impossible as a science. For while there is a method (transcendental deduction) of validating transcendental knowledge-claims, there is no comparable method of validating transcendent knowledge-claims.

Instances of rationalist metaphysics include Descartes' dualism of *res cogitans* and *res extensa*, Spinoza's monism of nature, and Leibniz's pluralism of monads. Kant sees each of these as an uncritical, i.e., transcendent, application of the category of substance. (We shall examine his critique of Descartes in the concluding section of this Part.) Other instances of rationalist metaphysics include the purported proofs—or refutations—of the existence of God, the freedom of the will, and the immortality of the soul. Kant sees these "proofs" and "refutations" as based on the uncritical applications of the principle of causality. We shall have a look at his critique of these attempts at transcendent knowledge in the following three sections.

God

Our only object of knowledge is the phenomenal world—the objective, empirical world studied by science. God, if he exists, would be the Creator of this world. But there can be no scientific proof of his existence. For example, we may not argue from the principle causality ("Every event has a cause") to the conclusion that the phenomenal world has a cause. For that principle has a justified application only *within* the phenomenal world.

Although the idea of an infinitely wise, good, and powerful Lord of the Universe does not function to represent a possible object of knowledge, it does, for Kant, have other meaningful employments. It is used to express the (for us) unattainable scientific ideal of a perfectly unified and unconditional comprehension of reality. And it is used to express our ethical faith in the real possibility of a Heavenly City—a world of perfect harmony between virtue and happiness. In other words: *theoretical reason* (science) postulates a God's eye-knowledge of reality as the ultimate, but humanly unattainable, goal of its own efforts, while *practical reason* (morality) postulates the existence of a Being powerful and good enough to guarantee that the virtuous will finally inherit the earth. Now Kant is prepared to admit that there are good reasons for believing in this all-knowing and providential Being, but he also stresses that these are reasons of a personal and practical nature,[20] and not the impersonal and theoretical reasons given by "rational theology" in its allegedly scientific proofs of God.[21]

Freedom

Since our only object of knowledge is the phenomenal world, freedom of the will cannot be an object of knowledge for us. Indeed, since every event in the phenomenal world is caused (necessitated by antecedent events in accordance with natural laws), no event in the phenomenal world can be free. For when we call a person free, we are thinking of her as a moral agent, i.e., as someone capable of acting on principle and determining her own actions by reasons; and so we are *not* regarding her as a mere phenomenal object, i.e., as someone merely reacting to stimuli in accordance with natural law.

We presuppose natural determinism when we investigate human behavior empirically. We presuppose freedom of the will when we regard human behavior from a moral point of view, judging it as virtuous or vicious. But the problem is that these two presuppositions seem to be contradictories. Some philosophers have tried to resolve this problem—this "dilemma of freedom and necessity," as it is called—by disproving one of the "contradictory" presuppositions. For example, Spinoza argued that free will (together with the ethics which presupposes it) are illusions, while Leibniz thought he could prove that natural necessitation is an illusion. But Kant rejects all of these arguments as so many vain attempts to achieve transcendent knowledge. We can know that the will *as object of empirical investigation* (as a phenomenal reality) is subject to causal laws, but we cannot know that the will *as it is in itself* (a noumenal, spiritual reality) is subject to the same laws.

For Kant, the resolution of the freedom/determinism dilemma is found in "the fact that we think of man in a different sense and relationship when we call him free from that in which we consider him as a part of nature and subject to its laws."[22] But this resolution must be clearly distinguished from Hume's reconciliation project. Hume argued that when we call a man free we are simply making the empirical claim that his behavior is unimpeded or uncoerced (e.g., that he is not in chains). If Hume is right, then a free act is a *caused* event, as much as any other event in nature. It's just that a free act is caused by factors *internal* to the agent (his desires and character traits), rather than by external factors. But if Kant is right, then it *is* contradictory to say that a man's behavior is both free and caused, *unless* we think of him "in a different sense and relationship when we call him free from that in which we consider him as a part of nature and subject to its laws." For Kant, when we call a person free we are going beyond any empirical claim and stepping outside of the conceptual framework of natural science and its causal laws: we are talking about the supersensible world governed by the laws of freedom, rather than about the phenomenal world of causal determinism. Although not an object of knowledge (a phenomenon), this supersensible (noumenal) world is a presupposition of moral action.

Immortality

The practical ethico-religious faith of much of mankind seems to involve the idea of an afterlife in which the souls of the dead meet their Maker and are judged by him. Kant shared this common practical faith but objected to attempts by rationalist philosophers to transform it into the conclusion of a theoretical proof. And thus he objected to Descartes' famous attempt to prove the separability of the soul from the body and the possibility of its post-mortem survival.

Descartes had argued that, since the subject of conscious states (the *I* in "I am thinking so and so") cannot be a material substance, it must be therefore an *immaterial* substance, an enduring spiritual substratum for those ever-changing conscious states. Kant objected that Descartes was here making an unwarranted application of the category of substance. We shall discuss this objection, along with some related matters, in the following section.

Critique of Cartesian Metaphysics

You will remember that Descartes developed his influential metaphysics of mind/body dualism through the following line of reasoning:

(1) I *am* directly aware of my own existence as a thinking substance (a mind).
(2) I am *not* directly aware of the existence of my body, or of any physical substance.

Therefore

(3) I, as a thinking substance, am really distinct from my body, and could exist in complete independence of it or of any physical thing.

Kant agrees that there is a radical distinction between mental states, such as ideas and sensations, and physical states, such as solidity and liquidity. The distinction, as he puts it, is that the former are present *in* time and present *to* "inner sense" (introspection), while the latter are present *in* space as well as time, and present *to* "outer sense" (sense perception). But Kant does not agree that it follows necessarily from this distinction that mental states and physical states inhere in different *substances*—in Descartes' *res cogitans* and *res extensa,* respectively. He grants, in effect, that Spinoza *may* have been right when he said that thought and extension are simply two aspects of one and the same underlying reality. It is *possible,* he says, that

> ... the substance which in relation to our outer sense possesses extension is in itself the possessor of thoughts, and that these thoughts can by means of its own inner sense be consciously represented. In this way, what in one relation is entitled corporeal would in another relation be at the same time a

thinking being, whose thoughts we cannot intuit [perceive], though we can indeed intuit their signs in the [field of] appearance. (A 359)

In this passage, Kant was focusing on the conclusion of Descartes' argument. Let us now consider what he has to say about the premises. We will see that, through his analysis of these premises, Kant was able to show that Cartesian dualism is rooted in two deep confusions: one about the nature of self-knowledge, the other about the nature of perception.

(1)

In the first premise of the argument under consideration, Descartes claimed to be aware of himself as *res cogitans,* i.e., as a thinking substance. It seems that, starting from a direct awareness of his own *changing, diverse, subjective states,* he inferred the existence of a *permanent, unified, subject* of those states—a solid channel, as it were, for his stream of consciousness.

Kant saw this inference as an unjustified application of the category of substance, an application based on a profound misinterpretation of the *unity of consciousness:*

> The unity of consciousness ... is here mistaken for an intuition of the subject as object, and the category of substance is then applied to it. But this unity is only unity in *thought,* by which alone no object is given, and to which, therefore, the category of substance, which always presupposes a given *intuition,* cannot be applied. (B 421–422)

This misinterpretation of the unity of consciousness is the root of what Kant calls rational [i.e., rationalistic] psychology. *Rational psychology* is the would-be *a priori* science of the soul which claims to demonstrate the separability of the soul from the body and the possibility of its immortal existence.

The unity of consciousness consists in the fact that the "I think" *(cogito)* must be able to accompany all of my thoughts, so that I can always know immediately that *this thought* and *that idea* are equally mine. Following Descartes at this point, Kant puts the matter as follows:

> The *"I think"* must be capable of accompanying all my ideas; for, otherwise, I should be conscious of something that could not be thought; which is the same as saying, that I should not be conscious at all, or at least should be conscious only of that which for me was nothing. (B 131, Watson trans.)

Later, Kant explains that this concept, this *I think* which introduces all our thought as belonging to consciousness, enables us

> ... to distinguish two objects within the nature of our faculty of representation. *I,* as thinking, am an object of the internal sense, and am called soul. That which is an object of the external senses is called body. (A 342/ B 400)[23]

Descartes had tried to deduce substantive conclusions about the soul from the concept of the "I (ego) which thinks." Kant's reply is that no substantive conclusion can be deduced from this concept, since it is nothing but a perfectly *empty* representation of a consciousness that accompanies all concepts:

> By this *I* . . . which thinks, nothing is represented beyond a transcendental subject of thoughts = *x*, which is known only through the thoughts that are its predicates, and of which, apart from them, we can never have the slightest concept, so that we are really turning round it in a perpetual circle, having already to use its representation, before we can form any judgment about it. And this inconvenience is really inevitable, because consciousness in itself is not so much a representation, distinguishing a particular object, but really a form of representation in general. . . . (A 346/ B 404, Müller trans.)[24]

Two substantive (i.e., synthetic) conclusions which Descartes claimed to deduce from the *cogito* are, (1) that the soul (ego) is a substance, and (2) that the soul could exist simply as a thinking thing, i.e., without a body. Let us conclude this subsection by looking at what Kant has to say about each of these two conclusions of Descartes' rational psychology:

> [1] That I, who think, can be considered in thinking as *subject only* . . . is an apodictical and even *identical* proposition [i.e., it is an analytic proposition]; but it does not mean that, as an object, I am a *self-dependent* being or a *substance*. The latter would be saying a great deal, and requires for its support data which are not found in the thinking. . . . (B 407, Müller trans.)
> [2] To say that I distinguish my own existence, as that of a thinking being, from other things outside me (one of them being my body) is likewise an analytical proposition; for *other* things are things which I conceive as *different* from myself. But, whether such a consciousness of myself is even possible without things outside me, whereby representations are given to me, and whether I could exist merely as a thinking being (without being a man), I do not know at all by that proposition.
> Nothing therefore is gained by the analysis of the consciousness of myself, in thought in general, towards the knowledge of myself as an object. The logical analysis of thinking in general is simply mistaken for a metaphysical determination of the object. (B 409, Müller trans.)[25]

(2)

In the second premise of his argument, Descartes says that he is *not* directly aware of the existence of any bodily thing. In saying this, he implies that mental states can be present to intuition, i.e., directly known, while physical things cannot be present to intuition and must therefore be known indirectly, i.e., by way of inference. It is for this reason that, at the end of the Second Meditation, he expresses the view that the mind is better known than the body.

The *existence* of the physical world, Descartes thought, must be inferred from the occurrence of ideas of sensation. But since he saw no intrinsic or necessary connection between ideas in the mind and objects in the world, he had to bring in an extrinsic cause (God) to explain the correlation of the one with the other. As for the *essence* of the physical world, i.e., its extension or spatiality, Descartes thought that it was present to intellectual (*a priori*) perception directly, as it is in itself. The essence of the physical world is open to the intuition of the intellect, though not to ocular vision.

According to Kant, the *existence* ("matter," contingent reality) of the physical world is directly presented to the mind empirically, in sensuous intuition. But he denies that the *essence* ("form," necessary structure) of the world is presented to the mind at all, i.e., given to it in any intuition. For, according to his Copernican revolution, the necessary structure (*a priori* form) of the world must be "ideal"—*contributed by the mind* itself, out of its own resources, rather than "real"—*given to the mind,* in intuition. What the mind, the knowing subject, contributes to the world in the act of knowing it is the *a priori* forms of sensuous intuition (space and time) and the *a priori* forms of understanding (the categories). We know that these forms apply to the world universally and necessarily. But we know this only because we have deduced that they are the universal and necessary forms of the world *as it is presented to us;* we do not know it because we have somehow perceived ("by an intuition of the intellect") the universal and necessary form of the world *as it is in itself.*

In short, for Kant *a priori* forms are only *conditions* of knowledge, whereas for Descartes they are also objects of knowledge. Descartes and the other rationalists thought of the human intellect as an intuitive power, having its own special, *noumenal* (supersensuous) objects.[26] But for Kant, it is only a concept-forming power, one which, when supplied with material from sensuous intuition, cognizes *phenomenal* (sensuous) objects.

Kant maintains *first,* that no knowledge is possible apart from a "measuring rod" (frame of reference); *second,* that this measure is supplied *by* the knowing subject, not supplied *to* him, in intuition; and *third,* that the measure supplied by the human knower consists in the spatio-temporal and categorial structure of his own mind.

Just as measuring the length of a table requires a measuring rod supplied by the measurer, so all perception of objective truth requires "criteria of being and truth"[27] supplied by the perceiver.

FROM THE
CRITIQUE OF PURE REASON

The reading for this chapter provides a valuable overview of the aims, methods, and conclusions of Kant's critical philosophy. Excerpted from Humphrey Palmer's new and lively translation and abridgement of the Critique of Pure Reason, *it contains key passages from the prefaces (the A and B, or First and Second Edition, Prefaces) and from the Introduction. The snappy (but somewhat misleading) title for this material, "Goodbye, Metaphysics!," is supplied by Professor Palmer.*

GOODBYE, METAPHYSICS![28]

1. What is Metaphysics?

A vii   Great problems confront us, unavoidable and yet insoluble: problems posed by the very nature of the mind, and yet beyond its powers to resolve.

Starting from principles which we have to rely on in ordinary life, we **A viii** work back to more fundamental laws—a never-ending task. Appealing then to axioms which go right outside experience and yet seem undeniable, we run into contradictions and obscurities. There must be a mistake somewhere; but as the axioms go beyond experience, they cannot be checked against experience. That is what metaphysical disputes are all about.

Time was, when Metaphysics reigned supreme among the sciences; and so she should, judging by the importance of her task. But times have changed. Rejected and forsaken, she now mourns like Ovid's Hecuba:

A ix   Once I was right at the top and ruled a great family,
Now I drag my life out in exile and in poverty.

Under the Dogmatists her government was despotic, until civil wars led to complete anarchy. The Sceptics (nomads they were, with no respect for permanent cultivation) repeatedly broke up all civil society; though each time it was rebuilt, all haphazard, there being fortunately few of them. Just lately it looked as if Locke might settle these disputes with his Mental Physiology. The "Queen", he said, was of common birth, born among the rabble **A x** of everyday experience. But his genealogy was forged. Back came the old moth-eaten Dogmatism, and down went Metaphysics, in the public eye. Having now tried everything (we think) and failed, we fall back on a weary Couldn't-Care-Less-ism: the mother of chaos and old Night, but perhaps also the harbinger of dawn.

But we do care, we must care about these things. For all their popular turns of speech, these Couldn't-Care-Less philosophers are in fact committed to metaphysical positions of their own. It is significant that this school **A xi** of thought should arise just when all the sciences are flourishing. Seeming-science is not current tender any more. People are calling for the mind to know itself—a most difficult task. They want an Inquiry, to confirm its **A xii** proper claims and reject the baseless ones, not by an arbitrary Fiat but by the unchanging laws that Reason always obeys. It is a *Critique of Pure Reason* they are looking for; not a critique of books or of systems of thought, but an assessment of the mind's own powers to know things *independently* of experience, to decide if Metaphysics is possible at all, and how far it can go.

A xiii   I have tried to make this complete, and venture to claim that every problem of Metaphysics has here been resolved, or at least the key provided for solving it.

A xiv   You may smile at these immodest claims; but I am claiming less than anyone who offers to prove that the soul is simple, or that the world must have once begun. He goes beyond all possible experience; I don't. I am dealing with the human mind—an item I should come across without travelling too far. Logic gives us a lead, with its list of all the basic operations of the mind. Our question is, how far can the mind go *without* the material and assistance of experience.

(1781)

2. *Scientific Progress in Logic*

B vii   In the field of Reason, is our knowledge progressing soundly, like a science? Let us look at the results. Everlasting stops and starts. Retreats and diversions. No agreement between those working in the field. That is not scientific progress, it is Blind Man's Buff. If only we could show Reason the way, what a benefit that would be, even at the cost of abandoning some ill-considered aims and claims.

viii   Logic has been going on safely, since antiquity. Never since Aristotle has it had to retrace a single step. It hasn't stepped forwards either, for it is complete. Extra chapters have no doubt been written, on where our thoughts come from (Imagination), on certainty about various things (Idealism, Scepticism, etc.), and on the causes and treatment of Prejudice. But they are out of place. The only business of Logic proper is to set out and establish

ix   the formal Laws of Thought. That is why Logic got on so well; it disregards the *objects* of knowledge, in all their infinite variety, and concentrates solely on the mind, studying the moves it makes. Reason, by contrast, will have a harder time getting onto the high road of Progress; for it deals with the objects as well, and not only with itself. Logic is just introductory: for real knowledge we must go to "the sciences".

3. *Progress in pure Science*

If Reason contributes to the sciences, they must contain an element known

x   "in advance" *[a priori]*. This pure element needs to be dealt with first.

Two rational sciences apply "in advance" to things, Mathematics and Physics. Mathematics is entirely pure, Physics partly so, but drawing on other sources of information as well.

xi   Mathematics was set on the path of progress by the Greeks. It had a prehistory (under the Egyptians) of hit-and-miss, before the Revolution altered everything. Whose that was we do not know. Diogenes Laertius, however, mentions a "discoverer" for each and every theorem of geometry; which shows that people realized that this method was new and important. Whoever (Thales?) worked out the properties of isosceles triangles must have

xii   "seen the light"; finding the answer did not come from the diagram, nor from the plain idea of "figure with three sides, two being equal": it had to be obtained by construction, from what he had thought into it at the start. Otherwise certainty is unobtainable.

Physics got off to a slower start. It is only a century and a half since Bacon's proposals led to and encouraged a rapid revolution. Think of Galileo rolling balls of known weight down a slope; of Torricelli making the air support a weight equal to a known column of water; of Stahl, later, turning metal to

xiii oxide and back again, by adding or subtracting a certain element; that is when the scientists saw the light, and realized that the mind can understand only what it has decided to produce. Nature does not doodle the mind along in baby-harness: it is the mind which leads the way and "puts Nature to the question". Observations made at random cannot produce a necessary Law of the sort we require. One needs rational principles (without which coincidence of observations would not lead to law) *plus* experiment (rationally designed according to those principles), in order to learn from Nature—not as a schoolboy, mind you, who believes everything the master says, but as a judge compelling a witness to reply. The mind contributes something of its

xiv own. What it cannot supply must be got from Nature; but what it gets must accord with what is supplied *to* Nature by the mind. That was the discovery which revolutionized physics and set it safely on the path of scientific progress, after so many centuries of hit-and-miss.

4. Non-progress in Metaphysics

Metaphysics is a rational, speculative science, quite separate from other sciences, deriving its information from concepts only, not experience (unlike Mathematics, which gets it by applying concepts *to* experience). It is the oldest of the sciences, and would survive if all the rest were destroyed in a new barbarism. But it has not found the way of progressive scientific development. It cannot establish the most basic laws of ordinary experience. Spe-

xv cialists in this field never agree, it is more like a battlefield—a stage battlefield, plenty of clatter and no real victories. It is all just hit-and-miss: *conceptual* hit-and-miss. Clearly the path of scientific progress has not yet been found.

xvi Mathematics and physics made the grade by a single revolution. Could metaphysics do the same?

5. A new approach required

The assumption has always been that knowledge should conform to its object. This rules out conceptual contributions "in advance". Then why not have objects conforming to our knowledge? Knowledge-in-advance should then be possible, something could be known about objects *before* they arrive.

One thinks of Copernicus' idea: that astronomy was stuck with a stationary observer and rotating stars, and might go further with a rotating observer

xvii and stationary stars. In metaphysics this goes for the stage of observation, of just seeing things ("intuition"). If the observation depends entirely on the object's properties then nothing about it can possibly be known-in-advance; as *could* happen, were the objects to depend (as seen or heard, etc.) on the properties of the observational equipment we deploy.

xix The experiment worked! It has put metaphysics on the path of progress, showing that advance-knowledge is possible of fundamental laws. It also

xx shows that metaphysics can never take us beyond experience, as it has always

claimed to do. Advance-knowledge, yes, but only of phenomena. How-
xxi Things-*really*-are is something *we* can never know (though action may give us
some inkling of what is Beyond and Behind everything).[29]
xxii Once started, metaphysics can soon complete its task. Its objects are
within, and interconnected, so that none can be known without knowing all
xxiv the rest as well. It deals with principles, and with the limits they prescribe
to their own employment. And it is basic to all the others, so it must be
finished first—"Nothing's done, we reckon, while anything is left to do".

Our Critique will seem, at first, to have only this negative result: that rational theorizing must not venture out beyond experience. Well, if it
shouldn't, it will pay us to know! But there is another side to this. When
xxv theorizing goes further it interferes with rational reflection on questions of
morality (by widening the world of sense, in effect, to include everything).
Preventing this interference is surely a positive service to morality—unless
you say that police work is entirely negative, since all they do is *prevent* citizens from assaulting other citizens.

The results are these: (1) Space and Time are just forms controlling sensible observation, so things-as-they-seem just have to be spatio-temporal. (2)
xxvi Rational concepts (on which some knowledge of Reality might have been
based) must all have observations to match; so nothing can be known as it
really is, but only as a sensible observation, as a "seem" [a phenomenon]. So
rational theorizing refers only to objects of experience. We can still *think*
xxvii about how-things-really-are. Otherwise there would be "seeming" but nothing there to seem!

6. *The real You is free*

Suppose you drop our distinction between how things seem and how they
really are. Mechanism and the law of universal causation would then apply
to simply everything. Man could not then be free *and* subject to natural necessity: that would be contradictory. Now bring back our distinction. Causal
law will apply only to how-things-seem, to objects of experience, not to those
objects taken as Reality. As-it-seems, then, the Will is not free, but subject to
xviii laws of nature in its visible actions. But as a Real Will it is free, and not
subject to those laws; though this real will can't be *known,* but only *thought.*
xxix Morality presupposes that the will is free. If theory showed this to be un-
thinkable, we should have to abandon morality and submit to Mechanism.
To save morality (and science) it needs to be shown that we just don't know
how-things-really-are. And that our Critique does show.

Theory cannot penetrate the Reality of things. But for this fact, one could
xxx not even *talk* about God, Freedom, or Immortal Life. Science had to be banished here to make room for faith.

7. *No-one will miss the bad old arguments*

The current dogmatism sets young folk on to waste their time chopping
xxxi logic and spinning theories on matters they do not understand—matters no-
one will ever understand—instead of studying the basic sciences. Our critique should put a stop to that. It will put an end once and for all to attacks
on religion and morality, in Socratic manner, by showing how little the at-
tackers know.

xxxii   There will be some loss, on paper, to the theorists, and to universities with their restrictive practices: not to humanity at large. Take the argument from simplicity of substance to the survival of the soul; take the distinction between subjective and objective compulsion, to save freedom for the Will; take the Ontological Argument; and ask yourself, my case-hardened dogmatist, whether they ever affect the public, outside school. People are moved by other factors, not by abstract argument. They expect life after death be-

xxxiii   cause life now, in time, has not satisfied them; they believe in freedom because they hear Duty's call; they believe in the Creator because of the order, beauty and thoughtful care they see around them in the world. Let universities concentrate on proofs everyone can understand, leaving the theorist in

xxxiv   sole charge of an esoteric but beneficial science, the Critique of Reason. That critique alone can eradicate Materialism, Fatalism, Atheism, freethinking disbelief, Fanaticism and Superstition, not to mention Idealism and

xxxv   Scepticism. A government concerned about the affairs of scholarship had much better back this critique, and put rational enquiry on a firm footing, instead of supporting those laughable college-autocrats who cry Public Danger when a cobweb gets destroyed.

There is no harm in dogmatic procedure in science, i.e. in proving things properly, from sound principles. But we are against dogmatism, i.e. proving things *from concepts alone*, in the same old way, without even asking what right we have to them. Dogmatism is the mind proceeding on its own, dogmatically, without first reckoning if it has the required powers.

xliii   This work is complete in principle. I shall value comments on it, but shall not engage in dispute, for my time is short. I am 63 this month, and still have to write a Metaphysic of Science and a Metaphysic of Ethics, to confirm that the Critiques of theorizing and of moralizing are correct.

(April 1787)

8. What experience cannot teach us must be given in-advance

1   Human knowledge all starts from experience. Things come in contact with our senses, yielding ideas and moving us to compare, connect or distinguish those ideas. We thus make up, from the raw material of sensible impressions, that finished knowledge of objects that is called Experience. Knowledge in humans, then, cannot occur *before* experience.

Does it follow that our knowledge is based entirely *on* experience? No. Even our knowledge of things involves two elements, one received as impres-

2   sions and the other provided by ourselves. It may take much skill and long practice to distinguish these.

Just what do we mean by "knowing-in-advance"? We might say, of someone who dug beneath his house, that he could have known what would happen *in advance*, i.e. without making the experiment! But then he already knew that bodies are heavy, and fall if you take away what holds them up: general facts which in their turn had to be learnt by experience. In this book, however, knowledge "in-advance" will mean knowledge independent of all experience, not just of this or that particular experience.

3   There are two indicators, for spotting instances of knowledge-in-advance: (1) We may know by experience that A is B, but not that it *has* to be. Must-be statements are based on some prior information, not on mere experi-

ence. (2) From experience of a series of instances we can generalize to "what usually happens"—which should strictly be prefaced with "Observation so
4 far has revealed ... ". For a statement of what *always* happens some "advance" information must have been required. These two indicators, *necessity* and *strict universality*, belong together but can be used independently.

Some scientific theories are both necessary and completely general, and so represent knowledge given "in advance"; mathematical theorems, for ex-
5 ample, or the principle that every change is caused. Metaphysical theories
7 also go right outside experience. That makes the subject much more difficult; but it seems too important to give up. Ultimate questions about God, human Freedom, and man's Immortality, are in consequence treated dogmatically, without first checking on our competence to answer them.

• • •

9. Statements are either analytic or informative

10 Those statements which connect a subject (A) to a predicate (B) may do so in either of two ways: (i) B is really, though not obviously, part of the concept A, or (ii) B although linked to A is no part of its concept. Statements of the first type I call "analytic"; the others could be called "informative" [synthetic]. In an analytic, explanatory statement the "is" indicates identity:
11 but in an informative, expansive statement A and B are different: you could never get to B just by analysing A. Thus "all bodies are extended" is analytic, since extension is part of the concept *body;* but "all bodies are heavy" is informative, since *body* and heaviness are quite distinct. Empirical statements are all informative. It would be silly to base an analytic judgment on experience; the concept alone is enough to go on, and the evidence of experience is not required. That a body is extended is something settled in advance of
12 experience, since the required information is already given in the concept. The case of heaviness is different. Heaviness is not part of the concept *body*. It is one aspect of an item of experience, connected by me with another aspect of that same experience. I can learn the characteristics of *body* by analysis: extension, impenetrability, shape, etc. But now I go further. Considering experience (from which the concept of *body* was derived), I find that its characteristics are always combined with heaviness: so I link this predicate to the concept. This statement is informative. Informative statements made in advance of experience, however, cannot have such assistance from experi-
13 ence. Thus in "every event has a cause", *event* implies a Being preceded by a certain Time, but does not include *cause*. How is it then that I come to see *cause* as linked necessarily to *event?* The linkage is not due to experience, being too general in application and regarded as necessary. Clearly it is something known in advance of experience.

10. Fundamental laws of Science are informative, but not empirical

14 Mathematical theorems are all informative in character—although the analytic nature of mathematical inference has made many think the principles it starts from must be analytic too. In fact, you need informative principles, to support informative theorems, even though the steps between are purely analytic and deductive in character.

Mathematical theorems, at least those of pure mathematics, are advance-knowledge, not empirical; for experience could never supply the necessity which they all display.

15 You might think that "7 + 5 = 12" is analytic. But "7 + 5" just indicates some number which 7 and 5 add up to, without saying what that number is. Analysis of the notion "7 + 5" will never yield "12". To get beyond the mere notion "7 + 5" you need sensible assistance, e.g. five fingers, to help add to

16 the 7 the units making 5.

You can push and pull your ideas about as much as you like, they won't do sums for you—try bigger numbers, if you think they will! Statements of arithmetic, then, are informative in character.

What about geometry? "A straight line is the shortest one between two points" is informative. For *straight* is a mere quality, and contains no quantity [like *short*]. So *shortest* is something extra, not obtainable by analysing "straight line". Suitable assistance is needed here also, to link *short* with *straight*. Geometers do use certain basic laws like "a = a" and "the whole is

17 greater than its part". These are analytic but are not really principles: the theorems are not based *on* them so much as proved *by means of* them.

The basic laws of physics are both informative and given in advance, e.g. "in all corporeal change the amount of Matter is unchanged". This principle is necessary, and therefore given in advance. Moreover the notion of Matter

18 does not include permanence, but only a presence occupying Space. So the principle goes beyond the mere notion of Matter, adding something further: it is *informative*.

11. *Metaphysics could do with principles like that*

Metaphysics may have been a failure so far, but we can't help trying to make a science out of it, which will need informative principles given in advance. It is not just a matter of analysing and explaining the notions we have formed of things in advance. We want to extend our knowledge, so we need principles which go beyond the given concept: so far beyond, indeed, that experience cannot always follow them, e.g. when it is said that the world must have begun once upon a time. Metaphysics, then, is at least *meant* to be based on informative principles given in advance.

20 In general terms, the problem is: how can statements be made which are both informative and given in advance? In particular, we shall also have to ask

How is pure mathematics possible?

How is pure physics possible?

Mathematics and physics are both there, so it must be all right to ask how they are possible—for the fact of their being there is proof enough that they

21 are possible! People do, however, question whether metaphysics is possible, since no system propounded so far has proved satisfactory. Metaphysics is of course there, in the sense that people always have and always will raise certain questions, unanswerable on the basis of experience, which they then try to settle by speculation and by reasoning. So we may well ask

22 *How come these metaphysical tendencies?*

But explaining the tendency is not enough. Questions like "Has the world a beginning?" always leads us to absurdities. Surely we can at least decide whether such questions are decidable; or whether there are certain limits, beyond which human reason is quite unreliable. So we must ask

How is scientific metaphysics possible?

12. What a Critique of Pure Reason can do for us

23   The critical assessment of our reason's powers is thus a sort of science; not a very big one, since it does not deal with the objects of reason, innumerable and various, but with reason itself. When reason has once recognized its own limited powers in regard to objects of experience, it can soon work out how far and how safely it can venture out beyond experience.

25   So there could be a special science called *The Critique of Pure Reason*, "reason" being the source of all principles known "in advance". By a critique I don't mean a list of all such principles, still less a system of them and their consequences, just an assessment of the sources and limits of such a system of principles. The main use of such a critique would be negative: not to extend our speculative knowledge, but to make it safer and clearer. It is a second-order enquiry, dealing not so much with objects as with our knowledge of them, i.e. with whether we can know such objects in advance. To ensure that the knowledge is all given in advance, we must exclude any concept even partially empirical. So although the basic principles and concepts of morality are known-in-advance, they cannot come in here, since questions of duty are bound to refer to matters of experience. Second-order or "transcendental" philosophy is thus a matter of speculative, not of practical reason.

FOR FURTHER READING

G. J. WARNOCK, "Kant," in D. J. O'Connor, ed., *A Critical History of Western Philosophy*. Glencoe, Ill: The Free Press, 1964. One of the best short overviews of Kant's thought in English. Another is:

W. H. WALSH's "Kant," in Paul Edwards, ed., *The Encyclopedia of Philosophy*, Vol. 4. New York: Macmillan, 1967.

ROGER SCRUTON, *Kant*. New York: Oxford University Press, 1982. A short but penetrating account of the critical philosophy.

RALPH WALKER, *Kant*. London: Routledge & Kegan Paul, 1979. A longer work, giving an interpretation of Kant's epistemology rather different from Scruton's.

JUSTUS HARTNACK, *Kant's Theory of Knowledge*. New York: Harcourt, Brace, & World, 1967. An exceptionally lucid account of the first *Critique*.

WILLIAM A. HARPER AND RALF MEERBOTE, eds., *Kant on Causality, Freedom, and Objectivity*. Minneapolis: University of Minnesota Press, 1984. Gordon Nagel's "Substance and Causality" (pp. 97–107) will be more accessible to the beginner than many of the other articles.

HENRY E. ALLISON, *Kant's Transcendental Idealism*. New Haven: Yale University Press, 1983. An outstanding recent interpretation and defense of Kantian epistemology. Difficult, though clearly written.

IMMANUEL KANT, *Prolegomena to Any Future Metaphysics*. Indianapolis: Hackett, 1977. One of Kant's shorter and more accessible works.

NORMAN KEMP SMITH, trans., *Immanuel Kant's "Critique of Pure Reason."* London: Macmillan, 1929. (Paperback edition: New York, St. Martin's, 1965.) The most frequently used translation.

HUMPHREY PALMER, *Kant's Critique of Pure Reason: An Introductory Text*. Cardiff, U.K.: University College Cardiff Press, 1983. An extensively edited and freshly translated version of Kant's great classic.

QUESTIONS

1. *Define:* judgment, knowledge, *a priori* knowledge, *a posteriori* knowledge, analytic judgments, synthetic judgments.

2. How is *a priori* knowledge of analytic truths possible?

3. How is *a priori* knowledge of synthetic truths possible? (Be sure to bring Kant's Copernican revolution into your answer.)

4. What are the *pure forms of intuition* and how do they relate to the *pure forms of the understanding?* What are *phenomena* and how do they relate to *things as they are in themselves?*

5. Summarize how Kant explained and justified the categories of substance and causality.

6. Is Kant's thesis that we have knowledge of things as they appear to us, not of things as they are in themselves, a form of skepticism?

7. What is metaphysics and what view does Kant take of its scope and limits? How does Kant's view compare with those of (a) rationalism, and (b) Hume?

8. Discuss Kant's resolution of the freedom/determinism problem, comparing it with Hume's.

9. Discuss Kant's critique of Descartes' rational psychology.

10. Briefly summarize Kant's position on each of the "Five Main Issues of Modern Philosophy," mentioned in Chapter 1.

11. The Conclusion of Kant's *Prolegomena,* entitled "On the Determination of the Bounds of Pure Reason," contains an interesting critique of Hume's *Dialogues* and a defense of theism. Study it carefully and then write an analysis of Kant's argument. Include a direct comparison of Philo's conception of religions language (*Dialogues,* II, pp. 14–15) with Kant's "symbolic anthropomorphism" (*Prolegomena,* Sec. 57).

NOTES

[1] This and the next quotation are from Walsh's "Categories," in Robert Paul Wolff, ed., *Kant* (Garden City, N.Y.: Doubleday, 1967), pp. 55–56.

[2] These tasks include that of describing the universal and necessary structure of the world.

[3] All references to the *Critique of Pure Reason* will be by means of the standard page numbers, which are found in the margins of most editions of the work. "A" refers to the First Edition, "B" to the Second Edition. The passages quoted are from Norman Kemp Smith's translation (New York: St. Martin's Press, 1965), unless otherwise noted. Quoted with permission of the publisher.

[4] Categorial = pertaining to categories.

[5] Cf. the last paragraph of Descartes' Sixth Meditation.

[6] From *Prolegomena,* 318–320. Translated by Paul Carns, with revisions by James W. Eddington (Indianapolis: Hackett, 1977), pp. 61–62.

[7] Kant's discussion of space and time is found in the "Transcendental Aesthetic" of the first *Critique,* and in the First Part of the *Prolegomena.* My exposition of this material is indebted to H. E. Matthews' "Strawson on Transcendental Idealism," *Philosophical Quarterly,* Vol. 19 (1969), pp. 204–220.

[8]See Chap. I of "Analytic of Concepts" in the first *Critique.*

[9]The relevant parts of the *Critique,* for this section and the next, are "The Deduction of the Pure Concepts of Understanding" (in Chap. II of the "Analytic of Principles") and "Analogies of Experience," especially the First and Second Analogies (in Chap. II of the "Analytic of Principles"). (See also the "Refutation of Idealism," B 275–279.) This material, though particularly important, is notoriously difficult; it has consequently given rise to widely different interpretations. I have not tried to give a play-by-play analysis of it, but only to convey its spirit.

[10]Cf. the "piece of wax" passage in the Second Meditation. Descartes seems to have anticipated parts of Kant's analysis of change—as did Aristotle, in *Physics,* I.

[11]I take this terminology from Gordon Nagel's "Substance and Causality," in W. A. Harper and R. Meerbote, eds., *Kant on Causality, Freedom, and Objectivity* (Minneapolis: University of Minnesota Press, 1984), pp. 97–107. And I am much indebted to Nagel's article for this whole section, both for what I say and how I say it.

[12]Locke's "passive powers of substances" correspond to Kantian "material properties." But it is unclear how Locke, as an empiricist, can claim to have any idea of these hidden powers. See the *Essay:* II, xxi, 1–4 (pp. 62–63 above).

[13]A common complaint of modern philosophers against the Scholastics was to say that they tended to postulate too many "occult," i.e., nonsensible entities and powers. Berkeley thought that Locke shared the same tendency.

[14]The concepts "potentiality" and "actuality" are associated with Aristotelian philosophy. But while Aristotle, and his Scholastic followers, said that these concepts are *abstracted from* sense experience, Kant would say that they are *prior conditions of* sense experience.

[15]In the *Treatise of Human Nature,* Hume had written that "the opinion of the necessity of a cause to every new production . . . must necessarily arise from observation and experience" (I,iii,3).

[16]This analysis is based on Henry Allison, *Kant's Transcendental Idealism* (New Haven: Yale University Press, 1983), pp. 222–228.

[17]Kant himself says that empirical judgments pertain to "things as they appear to us" (phenomena), not to "things as they are in themselves." But he wants to distinguish this position from the skepticism found in Descartes' First Meditation. (See *Critique,* A 27, B 274–75.) He rejects the "evil genius" assumption that all empirical judgments are, or could be, *illusory.* (See B 69–71.)

[18]The parts of the *Critique* that relate to the foregoing section of this book are the "Transcendental Deduction" and, especially, the "Refutation of Idealism."

I have been influenced in the way I read Kant by several Wittgensteinian writings, including F. Waisman's *The Principles of Linguistic Philosophy* (London: Macmillan, 1965), Chap. 2, Donald Screen's *Realism and Grammar* (University of Virginia dissertation, 1983), and O. K. Bouwsma's "Descartes' Evil Genius" (see reference in Chapter 1). I am especially indebted to Screen's work.

[19]From a translation by John Watson in Benjamin Rand, ed., *Modern Classical Philosophers* (Cambridge, Mass.: Houghton Mifflin, 1924), pp. 404–405.

[20]On this point, see W. H. Walsh's article on Kant in the *Encyclopedia of Philosophy* (New York: Macmillan, 1967), Vol. 4, p. 317.

[21]Kant's critique of rational (rationalistic) theology occurs in the section of the first *Critique* called "The Ideal of Pure Reason." I touched on it in my discussion of Hume, pp. 110–112.

I have drawn on material in H. E. Matthews' article (cited earlier) both in the preceding and in the following section.

[22]From "On the Extreme Limit of All Practical Philosophy," in the Third Section of Kant's *Foundations of the Metaphysics of Morals.* I have used L. W. Beck's translation. The *Critique of Pure Reason* discusses the freedom/determinism problem in the section entitled "The Antinomy of Pure Reason."

[23]F. Max Müller, trans. (New York: Macmillan, 1896).

[24]Compare with Sec. 27 of the *Principles,* where Berkeley says "there can be no idea [representation] formed of a soul or spirit."

[25]This, and most of the other passages quoted in this subsection, are from the part of the *Critique* called "The Paralogisms [fallacious inferences] of Pure Reason."

[26]For the Aristotelians, noumenal features ("intelligible species") were *hidden* in the phenomenal features ("sensible species") of things. They posited an active power ("active intel-

lect") which "irradiates" the sensible species of things, thereby making their underlying intelligible form visible to the intuitive power of the intellect ("passive intellect").

The rationalists were closer to Plato than to Aristotle in their account of "noumenal knowledge." Plato, Aristotle's teacher, argued that it cannot be derived from sense experience, and that it must be therefore an innate possession of the soul.

[27]I have borrowed this phrase (with modifications) from Leibniz (see p. 41, above). What Leibniz failed to see, according to Kant, was that these criteria are synthetic *a priori* laws which are prescribed to nature rather than derived from it. (See the section in Part One on Kant's Copernican revolution.)

[28]Reprinted with the kind permission of the publisher from Humphrey Palmer, *Kant's Critique of Pure Reason: An Introductory Text* (Cardiff, U.K.: University College Cardiff Press, 1983), Chapter I.

[29]Moral action—"acting out of a sense of duty"—suggests the reality of a realm of freedom "beyond or behind" the causal determinism of the phenomenal world. (W.H.B.)

retrospect

DESCARTES THROUGH KANT

The early modern philospher-scientists developed a certain picture of the essence of nature and of natural science. According to this picture, nature is a machine made up of many lesser machines; understanding nature, or some part of it, would be like tracing the mechanism of a clock. Tracing out the mechanism of something allows us to see the causes that determine its operation. The only real causality is *contact causality,* as when one gear moves another; to understand an event in terms of this causality allows us to see how it is a necessary outcome of antecedent conditions.

This picture was fervently embraced by a contemporary of Descartes, the Englishman Thomas Hobbes. Hobbes regarded mechanics, the science of bodies in motion, as *the* truth about reality. Few other modern thinkers accepted the mechanistic picture so unreservedly or unqualifiedly, although all were influenced by it in one way or another.

While describing "the whole visible universe in the manner of a machine, having regard only to the shape and movement of its parts,"[1] Descartes insisted on the distinct reality of the "invisible universe" of his own mind. "He could not accept, as Hobbes accepted, the claim that human nature differs only in degree of complexity from clockwork."[2] But Descartes' conception of the human mind as something essentially distinct and different from the rest of nature gave rise to the mind/body problem, and to the problem of knowledge. How can mind interact with the material world if it shares none of the latter's spatial and mechanical properties? And how can the mind gain knowledge of nature if it cannot interact with it?

Spinoza argued the intriguing, but paradoxical thesis that mind and body are two Attributes of one and the same reality, Substance. We and everything else exist in, and are to be understood in terms of, this one, infinite Substance, which is also called God or Nature. Nature is a thoroughly deterministic system, a system intelligible *either* in terms of mechanical laws *or* in terms of parallel and equally strict laws of psychology.

Spinoza rejected two features of Descartes' philosophy which were to capture the imagination of most modern thinkers: first, the individualistic starting point in the subjective certainty of the first person, present tense assertion, "I am thinking, therefore I exist"; second, the dualistic conception of the mind as really separable from body, and of body as soulless mechanism. Subsequent thinkers were either to retain in some form both of these features of Cartesian philosophy, or else to champion one side of the mind/body dualism at the expense of the other. The champions of body were called materialists; the champions of mind, idealists.

Leibniz was an idealist. While accepting the validity of the mechanistic picture at the phenomenal level, as the proper representation of the world of the senses, he rejected it at the noumenal level, as the true representation of the ultimate nature of reality. He tells us that the ultimate nature of reality is to be represented not in terms of the motion of atoms in space, but in terms of a hierarchy of "spiritual atoms" or "monads," monads being nonextended centers of life, each developing according to a law intrinsic to itself.

Locke was neither an idealist nor a materialist, but a dualist. He argued, however, for a modified and qualified version of the original Cartesian doctrine: (1) Rejecting the doctrine of innate ideas, Locke claimed that the materials of human knowledge come from human experience and that none of them are given to the mind directly by God.[3] (2) He allowed that bodies may operate by a principle distinct from contact causality, namely gravity or "action at a distance." Locke accepted this important modification of the mechanistic picture because experience, and the Newtonian system, seemed to require it; he accepted it reluctantly because he thought it involved attributing an unintelligible operation to matter.[4] (3) He introduced a note of cautious skepticism concerning dualist metaphysics, arguing that it is *possible* that matter thinks, even though we cannot understand *how* that is possible. "God can, if He pleases, superadd to matter a faculty of thinking" (*Essay:* IV, iii, 6). Although this view is very far from the gross materialism of Hobbes (according to which the brain secretes thought as the liver secretes bile!), it was far enough from the conventional piety of the time to be regarded as a "hideous hypothesis."[5]

Berkeley challenged the very popular version of the mechanistic picture presented by Newton and Locke. A thoroughgoing idealist in metaphysics and an instrumentalist in philosophy of science, he denied the real
existence of the invisible corpuscles (atoms) postulated by those philosophers. He also rejected that key element of modern philosophy, the distinction between the mind-dependent secondary qualities and the supposedly
mind-independent primary qualities of objects. Appealing to the empiricist
principle that there is nothing in the intellect that was not first in sensation,
Berkeley argued that to talk of "unsensed, mind-independent objects" is to
use words with no intelligible content.

Hume wanted to be the "Newton of the human mind." Arguing that
the psychological world of thoughts and feelings operate in accordance with
a few principles ("laws of association") just as bodies move in accordance
with a few principles (Newton's laws of motion), he maintained that there
is as much causal necessity in the former "world" as in the latter, and that
consequently there can be a science of psychology as well as of physics.
Judgments of causal necessity, Hume continues, are in every case based on
"custom," the natural, human tendency to project on to the future regularities experienced in the past. There is no case—not even the contact causality involved in the motion of clockwork—in which genuinely causal judgments are based on a clear and distinct perception of (quasi-mathematical)
connections between objects.

The tendency of the human imagination to project its feelings and
sentiments onto external objects was a topic of particular importance for
Hume. He illustrates some "trivial" manifestations of it in a rather mischievous passage:

> ... [A]mong all the instances wherein the Peripatetics [Aristotelians] have
> shown they were guided by every trivial propensity of the imagination, no
> one is more remarkable than their "sympathies," "antipathies," and "horrors
> of a vacuum." ... This inclination, it is true, is suppressed by a little reflec-
> tion, and only takes place in children, poets, and the ancient philosophers. It
> appears in children by their desire of beating the stone which hurt them; in
> poets by their readiness to personify everything; in the ancient philosophers
> by these fictions of sympathy and antipathy. (*Treatise:* I, iv, 3)

Hume goes on to claim that, while moderns as well as ancients rely on principles of the imagination, the moderns rely on principles which are "permanent, irresistible, and universal (such as the customary transition from
causes to effects)," in contrast with the "changeable, weak, and irregular"
principles of the ancient philosophers (I, iv, 4). Now, according to Hume,
the "fundamental principle of modern philosophy" is that colors and the
other secondary qualities are really impressions of the mind, derived from
the operation of external objects but with no resemblance to actual qualities
in objects. But though this opinion was instrumental in the development of

a new and powerful physics, it has an ironic and embarassing implication. For if the secondary qualities are nothing but perceptions of the mind, it follows that "nothing we can conceive is possessed of real, continued, and independent existence, not even motion, extension, and solidity, which are the primary qualities chiefly insisted on [by modern philosophers and physicists]" (I, vi, 4). This sort of reasoning led Berkeley to idealism (or "immaterialism," as he called it)—a doctrine regarded by Hume as "admitting of no answer and producing no conviction" (*EHU:* XII,1). "We may well ask, 'What causes induce us to believe in the existence of body?' but it is vain to ask, 'Whether there be body or not?' That is a point we must take for granted in all our reasonings" (*Treatise:* I, iv, 2).

"Two things fill the mind with ever new and increasing admiration and awe, the oftener and more steadily we reflect on them: *the starry heavens above and the moral law within.*" Thus begins the concluding section of Kant's *Critique of Practical Reason.* "The starry skies above" symbolize the inexorable, impersonal order of the world-machine; "the moral law within" is the realm of freedom and the moral law—the part of human life not within the scope of mechanical explanation. In order to reconcile these two realms, Kant limited application of the mechanistic picture to Appearances (phenomena), thereby leaving room for moral faith, i.e., for the practical conviction that, at the level of Reality (noumena, things in themselves), the will is free and the moral law efficacious. In this, Kant is in harmony with Leibniz. The big difference between them is that Kant, in opposition to Leibniz and all rationalists, denies the possibility of *knowing* any substantial truth about the noumenal realm. Included in this noumenal realm is God, the unified Source of the starry skies above and the moral law within. While agreeing with Hume's contention that we can have no substantive knowledge of such a Source, Kant insists on the practical, moral necessity of believing in it nonetheless.

Kantian epistemology may be the most ingenious and involved philosophical structure ever constructed. Partly for that reason interpretations of it differ, but most interpreters would probably accept something like the following as a sketch of its essentials: Whatever is given to us as an object of knowledge is (contrary to rationalism) given by means of the senses. But the senses never allow us to know things absolutely, as they are in themselves (as God would know them), but only relatively, in terms of the ideas through which they affect us. All the qualities of objects (primary as well as secondary), together with the space in which they exist, are mere appearances, i.e., representations in us existing nowhere but in our ideas.[6]

All of our claims to knowledge are (to continue the sketch) made from the standpoint of human sensibility. Space is not an object sensed but a *form* of sensibility. That form determines both the type of object judged and the type of quality it is judged to have. Therefore the truth about the external world—about the realm of objects in space—is internal to the human way of perceiving things. Only because we understand that *this* is what "truth about the external world" amounts to can we finally exorcise the ghost of skepticism first conjured up by Descartes' meditations. In other words: Kant resolved the problem of knowledge by reducing the truth about the world to something internal to our way of viewing it; he overcame philosophical skepticism by limiting knowledge-claims to objects of experience formed by the mind in accordance with principles of its own. This—Kant's Copernican revolution—is a continuation and radicalization of that "turn to the subject" found at the beginning of modern philosophy in Descartes' *Cogito ergo sum*. The secure foundation of the sciences, located by Descartes in the mind's consciousness of itself as the creation of a nondeceiving Deity, becomes, in Kant, the mind's consciousness of itself as an autonomous, world-constituting ("transcendental") ego.[7]

Can room be made in our philosophy for freedom and moral values without reducing nature to mere appearance? How much, if at all, does a genuine science of nature need to employ the "mechanistic picture"? To what extent are the Kantian categories universal and necessary principles of knowledge? Can philosophical skepticism be refuted without reducing the truth about nature to something internal to our way of viewing it? Was the "turn to the subject" by which Descartes initiated modern philosophy a *wrong* turn? Questions of this sort have been prominent in post-Kantian modern philosophy.

NOTES

[1]Descartes' *Principles of Philosphy,* Part IV, clxxxviii.

[2]Gilbert Ryle, *The Concept of Mind* (New York: Barnes & Noble, 1949), p. 19.

[3]Locke's campaign against this epistemological thesis was paralleled by his campaign against the political doctrine of the divine right of kings.

[4]In the *Essay* Locke had said that "bodies act by impulse, and nothing else" (II, viii, 2); he retracted this in a reply to a letter by a certain Bishop of Worcester, Edward Stillingfleet.

[5]On this and the preceding point, see Leibniz's fascinating critique in the Preface of his *New Essays on Human Understanding.*

[6]This is based largely on the *Prolegomena*, Remark II of the First Part.

[7]The preceding paragraph owes a very great deal to J. D. Kenyon's review of recent books on skepticism in *Philosophical Investigations,* Vol. 10 (1987), pp. 246–260. Incidentally, that same volume contains a fascinating article on the influence of the "mechanistic picture" on Tolstoy's conception of history in *War and Peace* (Richard Wood, "The Befuddled Hedgehog," pp. 173–199).

appendix

A SHORT TABLE
OF HISTORICAL DATES

1517	Luther's Ninety-Five Theses: beginning of the Reformation
1543	Copernicus' *The Revolutions of Heavenly Bodies:* beginning of the scientific revolution
1588	Defeat of the Spanish Armada; flourishing of Elizabethan England
1607	Founding of the first English colony in North America, at Jamestown, Virginia
1632	Galileo's *Dialogue Concerning the Two Chief World Systems*
1633	Galileo condemned by the Holy Inquisition
1637	Descartes' *Discourse on Method*
1648	Peace of Westphalia: end of the Thirty Years War
1649	Execution of Charles I of England
1661	Beginning of Louis XIV's rule of France
1677	Spinoza's *Ethics*
1684	Leibniz publishes his discovery of the infinitesimal calculus (he made the discovery in 1675; Newton had discovered it nine years earlier, but did not publish)
1687	Newton's *Principia:* climax of the scientific revolution
1688–89	"The Glorious Revolution" in England: parliamentary supremacy confirmed
1690	Locke's *Essay*
1710	Berkeley's *Principles*
1739–40	Hume's *Treatise*
1740	Accession of Frederick the Great in Prussia
1776	American Declaration of Independence; Adam Smith's *The Wealth of Nations*
1781	Kant's *Critique of Pure Reason*
1787	U.S. Constitution
1789	The French Revolution begins
1799	Napoleon comes to power in France

INDEX

Fanatic, 114
Final causes, 3, 14, 29, 33–35, 42, 50–51
First person, present tense assertion, 12, 150
Fitness, 48
Formal cause, 3
Franklin, Benjamin, 74
Frederick the Great, 155
Free cause, 30, 33
Freedom, 133, 143, 152
Freedom and determinism, 17, 98–100, 117, 133. *See also* Liberty and necessity.
Free will, 33, 36, 39, 99, 141, 152

Galileo Galilei, 2–8, 23, 41, 103, 140, 155
Geller, Uri, 102
Geometry, 9, 30, 39, 105, 144. *See also* Mathematics.
God, 2, 18, 29–30, 33–38, 42, 46–52, 55–56, 69, 77, 101, 103, 105–16, 143, 150, 152
God, arguments or proofs for,
  argument from contingency (Leibniz), 46
  cosmological arguments, 110–12. *See also* Locke's (below).
  design argument, 105, 107–10, 112–17, 142
  argument from eternal truths (Leibniz), 47
  Locke's argument, 56, 69
  ontological argument, 15, 23, 42, 105, 110–12, 142
  trademark argument, 13–14, 23
Good and bad, 36
Goodness, 17, 112
Grace, kingdom of, 51
Gravity, 78, 150. *See also* Heaviness.
Great deceiver. *See* Evil.
Greeks, the, 139

Habit, 45, 94, 97
Harmony, 37, 50, 51
Heat, 23–24, 36, 83
Heavenly City, 132. *See also* City of God.
Heaviness, 4, 18–19, 143
Hobbes, Thomas, 8, 149–50
Homogeneous system, 39
Hume, David, 90–118, 120–21, 133, 147, 151, 155

Idealism, 75, 79–81, 139, 142, 152
Idealists, 41, 150–51
Ideal structure, 137

Ideas, 6, 13, 58–59, 76, 79, 82, 103
  clear and distinct, 15, 17, 20–21, 63–64
  complex, 61–62
  compound, 91
  formal and objective reality of, 24
  inherent and representative reality of, 13, 24
  innate, 58, 92–93
  of reflection, 55, 59, 61
  of sensation, 55, 59–60, 88
  simple, 55, 60, 91
Illusory perception, 130, 147
Imagination, 34, 36–37, 71, 81, 88, 95, 97, 118, 151
Immaterialism, 75–77, 126. *See also* Idealism.
Immortality, 117, 134–35, 143. *See also* Soul, survival of.
Impressions, 91
  of sensation and reflection, 96
Inconceivability argument, 81
Incorrigibility, 12
Inductive arguments, 94–95. *See also* Experimental reasoning.
Infinity, 12
Instinct, 94
Instrumentalism, 78, 151
Intellect, active and passive, 147–48
Interactionism, dualistic, 24
Intuition, 67, 69, 124, 131, 137, 140

Jefferson, Thomas, 74
Jesus, 101
Johnson, Dr. Samuel, 89
Judgments, 13, 20
  analytic, 121
  of experience, 129
  illusory, 147
  logical forms of, 125
  synthetic, 121

Kant, Immanuel, 15, 74, 110–11, 119–148, 152–53, 155
Kierkegaard, Søren, 102
Knowledge, 1, 11, 58, 64–72, 121. *See also* A *priori* knowledge and a *posteriori* knowledge.
  demonstrative, 57
  innate, 147
  moral, 68
  problem of, 150. *See also* Perceptions, problem of.
  rational, sensitive, and intuitive, 67
  speculative, 147
  transcendental and empirical, 123